A Concise Guide to the
Level 3 Award in
Education & Training

You might also like the following books from Critical Publishing:

The A-Z Guide to Working in Further Education
Jonathan Gravells and Susan Wallace
978-1-909330-85-6 Published 2013

A Complete Guide to the Level 4 Certificate in Education and Training: 2nd Edition
Lynn Machin, Duncan Hindmarch, Sandra Murray and Tina Richardson
978-1-910391-09-9 Published 2015

A Complete Guide to the Level 5 Diploma in Education and Training: 2nd Edition
Lynn Machin, Duncan Hindmarch, Sandra Murray and Tina Richardson
978-1-910391-78-5 June 2016

Equality and Diversity in Further Education
Sheine Peart
978-1-909330-97-9 Published 2014

Inclusion in Further Education
Lydia Spenceley
978-1-909682-05-4 Published 2014

The Professional Teacher in Further Education
Keith Appleyard and Nancy Appleyard
978-1-909682-01-6 Published 2014

Reflective Teaching and Learning in Further Education
Nancy Appleyard and Keith Appleyard
978-1-909682-85-6 Published 2015

Teaching and Supporting Adult Learners
Jackie Scruton and Belinda Ferguson
978-1-909682-13-9 Published 2014

Teaching in Further Education: The Inside Story
Susan Wallace
978-1-909682-73-3 Published 2015

Understanding the Further Education Sector: A Critical Guide to Policies and Practices
Susan Wallace
978-1-909330-21-4 Published 2013

Our titles are also available in a range of electronic formats. To order please go to our website www.criticalpublishing.com or contact our distributor, NBN International, 10 Thornbury Road, Plymouth PL6 7PP, telephone 01752 202301 or email orders@nbninternational.com.

A Concise Guide to the
Level 3 Award in Education & Training

LYNN MACHIN, DUNCAN HINDMARCH,
SANDRA MURRAY, TINA RICHARDSON & FIONA HALL

First published in 2016 by Critical Publishing Ltd

British Library Cataloguing in Publication Data
A CIP record for this book is available from the British Library

ISBN: 978-1-910391-66-2

This book is also available in the following e-book formats:

MOBI ISBN: 978-1-910391-67-9
EPUB ISBN: 978-1-910391-68-6
Adobe e-book ISBN: 978-1-910391-69-3

The rights of Lynn Machin, Duncan Hindmarch, Sandra Murray, Tina Richardson and Fiona Hall to be identified as the Authors of this work have been asserted by them in accordance with the Copyright, Design and Patents Act 1988.

Text design by Greensplash Limited
Cover design by Out of House Ltd
Project Management by Out of House Publishing
Printed and bound in Great Britain by Bell & Bain, Glasgow

Critical Publishing
152 Chester Road
Northwich
CW8 4AL
www.criticalpublishing.com

Contents

Acknowledgements

We would like to thank our families, friends and colleagues for the support that they have given us during the writing of this book.

We would also like to thank our publishers, Julia Morris and Di Page, for their friendliness, professionalism and ongoing support.

Thanks also to you for reading this book. We hope that you enjoy reading it and best wishes with your studies.

Lynn, Duncan, Sandra, Tina and Fiona, 2016

Meet the authors

Lynn Machin is an award leader and senior lecturer. She is also a supervisor for students undertaking doctoral studies within the School of Education at Staffordshire University. She has more than 25 years' experience of working within further and higher education. Many of these years have been spent designing and delivering Initial Teacher Training for trainees who work, or want to work, in the further education sector. Her current research interests are situated in the exploration of how students can develop their capacities to learn and grow as self-directed and autonomous learners. As well as having written and co-authored several books for teachers within further education including *A Complete Guide to the Level 5 Diploma in Education and Training* and *A Complete Guide to the Level 4 Certificate in Education and Training*, Lynn has also written several other books including *Supporting Primary Teaching and Learning* (aimed at teaching assistants).

Duncan Hindmarch is award leader for and senior lecturer within the School of Education at Staffordshire University. With a background in teaching English for Speakers of Other Languages (ESOL), he has over 17 years of teaching experience. Duncan is a Senior Fellow of the Higher Education Academy and has led development and implementation of ESOL, Initial Teacher Training and Education programmes. As well as having written and co-authored several books for teachers within further education including *A Complete Guide to the Level 5 Diploma in Education and Training* and *A Complete Guide to the Level 4 Certificate in Education and Training*, Duncan has also written several other books including *Supporting Primary Teaching and Learning*.

Sandra Murray is a lecturer within the School of Education at Staffordshire University. Sandra, having taught for many years in a further education college, has a wide range of experience supporting and teaching teachers in the further education sector and has been teaching on Initial Teacher Education programmes since 2006. Her particular research interest is inspirational and outstanding teaching. She has written and co-authored several books for teachers within further education, including *A Complete Guide to the Level 5 Diploma in Education and Training* and *A Complete Guide to the Level 4 Certificate in Education and Training*.

Tina Richardson is an award leader and senior lecturer within the School of Education at Staffordshire University. Tina has taught in compulsory education, further education and higher education. For the last 15 years, she has been involved in teacher training for further education, in particular the subject specialist qualifications for teachers. Her particular research interest is the use of metacognitive reading strategies in the Functional Skills classroom. As well as teacher training books, including *A Complete Guide to the Level 5 Diploma in Education and Training* and *A Complete Guide to the Level 4 Certificate in Education and Training*, Tina has co-authored a book on using e-readers in the classroom.

Fiona Hall is an award leader for the BA in Education within the School of Education at Staffordshire University. She has more than 20 years' experience of working within primary, further and higher education. She has also been involved in teacher training in further education, undertaking teacher observations. Her current research interests are situated in the exploration of teaching assistant practice in schools. Fiona has co-authored *Supporting Primary Teaching and Learning*.

You will find more information about the authors and their research areas, as well as useful information about the further and higher education sectors, on their website: **www.teachwriteresearch.com**.

Preface

ABOUT THIS BOOK AND WHAT EACH CHAPTER COVERS

Training to be a teacher within the further education (FE) and skills sector can be an exciting and transforming learning experience. Studying for a level 3 Award in Education and Training (AET) is part of that process of transformation. The intention of this book is to support you in your studies as you make this transition and as you work towards achieving your AET qualification. It does this through:

○ coverage of all of the core units that are in the level 3 AET qualification;

○ alignment of chapters to the standards underpinning the level 3 AET qualification;

○ encouraging you to reflect upon your practice;

○ providing case study scenarios and examples;

○ indicating sources of information for further in-depth study;

○ being research informed and written by teacher educators with trainee teachers' needs in mind.

The topics, questions and activities within each chapter of this book have been tailored to the demands of the AET qualification and are aligned to the standards framework that can be found on the Education Training Foundation (ETF) website. You will find a table at the beginning of the book that shows which standards each of the chapters covers. In addition to this, in this book there is a chapter that focuses on helping you to develop your study skills, including advice about reading critically, note-taking, presenting your work, referencing correctly and assignment writing.

Each chapter begins by providing a visual concept map of the topics to be covered as well as a list of the chapter's objectives. Points for reflection are followed by detailed text accompanied by questions and activities that will provide you with an opportunity to check your understanding and assess your learning. Case studies bring the text to life and show how the theory can be applied in practice. At the end of each chapter you will find a summary of the main ideas and suggestions for further reading. At the back of the book you will find a helpful glossary of acronyms and useful examples of key templates that are used by teachers who work in FE.

What each chapter covers

The introduction and the chapters in this book cover the following topics.

Introduction

This provides you with a succinct overview of how policy has influenced the development of the FE sector. In particular, it provides you with a backdrop to the implementation, purpose and requirements of the AET.

Chapter 1: Understanding roles, responsibilities and relationships

This chapter focuses on your roles and responsibilities as a teacher. It introduces you to some of the legislation and regulations that you will need to be aware of as a teacher in the FE sector; for example, the Equality Act (2010).

Chapter 2: Understanding inclusive teaching and learning

This chapter provides you with information about how to engage all learners in activities as well as how and why different approaches to teaching and learning should be utilised.

Chapter 3: Facilitating learning and development for individuals

This chapter concentrates on the importance of tutorials, learning outside of the classroom and working in a classroom on individual activities.

Chapter 4: Facilitating learning and development in groups

This chapter explores some of the concepts of learning in groups, ways of facilitating learning and managing behaviour when learners are working in groups. It also identifies a few of the theoretical frameworks that support this method of learning.

Chapter 5: Principles and practices of assessment

This chapter outlines purposes, principles and practices of assessment. It develops understanding of the vital role assessment plays in informing learners, teachers, your institution and other relevant stakeholders of progress and future development needs.

Chapter 6: The microteach

This chapter draws together information from the other chapters and gives you guidance about preparing lesson plans and activities, delivering a session, formatively assessing learning and managing behaviour in the classroom.

Chapter 7: Essay writing

This chapter provides you with guidance about essay writing and developing your study skills. As well as the provision of practical examples it contains exercises that you can try out either on your own or with others in your group. This chapter also provides you with information about possible progression routes.

Links to the Education Training Foundation Professional Standards

Table 1 Chapter links to the ETF Professional Standards

STANDARDS*		CHAPTER
Professional values and attributes *Develop your own judgement of what works and does not work in your teaching and training*		
1.	Reflect on what works best in your teaching and learning to meet the diverse needs of learners	Chapters 1, 4, 6
2.	Evaluate and challenge your practice, values and beliefs	Chapters 1, 6
3.	Inspire, motivate and raise aspirations of learners through your enthusiasm and knowledge	Chapters 1, 2, 6
4.	Be creative and innovative in selecting and adapting strategies to help learners to learn	Chapters 1, 2, 3, 4, 6
5.	Value and promote social and cultural diversity, equality of opportunity and inclusion	Chapters 1, 2, 4
6.	Build positive and collaborative relationships with colleagues and learners	Chapter 1
Professional knowledge and understanding *Develop deep and critically informed knowledge and understanding in theory and practice*		
7.	Maintain and update knowledge of your subject and/or vocational area	Chapter 7
8.	Maintain and update your knowledge of educational research to develop evidence-based practice	Chapter 7
9.	Apply theoretical understanding of effective practice in teaching, learning and assessment, drawing on research and other evidence	Chapter 5
10.	Evaluate your practice with others and assess its impact on learning	Chapter 6
11.	Manage and promote positive learner behaviour	Chapters 1, 2, 4
12.	Understand the teaching and professional role and your responsibilities	Chapter 1
Professional skills *Develop your expertise and skills to ensure the best outcomes for learners*		
13.	Motivate and inspire learners to promote achievement and develop their skills to enable progression	Chapters 2, 3, 4
14.	Plan and deliver effective learning programmes for diverse groups or individuals in a safe and inclusive environment	Chapters 1, 3, 4, 6
15.	Promote the benefits of technology and support learners in its use	Chapter 5
16.	Address the mathematics and English needs of learners and work creatively to overcome individual barriers to learning	Chapters 2, 7
17.	Enable learners to share responsibility for their own learning and assessment, setting goals that stretch and challenge	Chapters 4, 5
18.	Apply appropriate and fair methods of assessment and provide constructive and timely feedback to support progression and achievement	Chapters 5, 6
19.	Maintain and update your teaching and training expertise and vocational skills through collaboration with employers	Chapter 1
20.	Contribute to organisational development and quality improvement through collaboration with others	Chapter 1

* Taken from the ETF (2014) standards.

Introduction: the further education and skills sector and the level 3 Award in Education and Training qualification

INTRODUCTION

If you have picked up this book then it is likely that you are either considering working in FE or that you have recently begun your career as a teacher, trainer, assessor or similar in FE. It is also likely to mean that you are studying for the level 3 AET qualification. This chapter develops your understanding of:

○ what has shaped the FE sector and led to the introduction of the level 3 AET qualification;

○ the implementation of the level 3 AET qualification;

○ the purpose of the level 3 AET qualification;

○ the requirements of the level 3 AET qualification.

WHAT'S IN A NAME?

You may be familiar with the term FE but you may not be as familiar with other terms given to the sector; for example, the lifelong learning sector (LLS) or post-compulsory education and training (PCET). PCET and the LLS broadly refer to post-compulsory education that takes place in a variety of settings (training organisations, hospitals, prisons, public organisations) whereas FE usually refers to post-compulsory education that takes place in a college environment. All of these terms refer to learners who are aged 16 (or, as relevant, post-14) and are in education and training. Literature, policies and reports use the terms post-compulsory, FE and LLS interchangeably. In the most recent documentation the name has again changed and the sector is now known as the further education and skills sector. For ease and brevity, this book will use the term FE throughout.

Similarly, differences in the names given to teacher training provision within FE also exist. These include Initial Teacher Training (ITT), Initial Teacher Education (ITE) and post-compulsory education and training (PCET). Again, for ease and brevity, the chapters in this book will use the term ITT.

WHAT IS THE FURTHER EDUCATION SECTOR?

There are more than four million learners currently engaged in learning in FE, all of whom will have their own reasons for wanting to study. For example, learners might need or want to develop their professional, crafts and vocational skills and knowledge or they might want to pursue a hobby or leisure activity. Sometimes the same course has learners who attend for professional development and learners who attend to develop a hobby; examples of such courses include hairdressing, language courses and motor mechanics. Courses are offered in a variety of settings, for example:

○   colleges (FE, sixth-form and special educational needs);

○   community learning and development;

○   higher education;

○   work-based learning.

Courses can be delivered to learners across a range of different abilities, for example pre-entry (below level 1) to higher education (level 7). You can find more information about award levels by looking at the Regulated Credit Framework (RCF) which, on 1 October 2015, replaced the Qualification Credit Framework (QCF); the web address for the RCF is in the reference section at the end of this introduction.

Due to the reliance on government funding and learners self-financing their education, courses offered year on year often vary; however, English, mathematics and ICT are always very popular.

WHAT HAS SHAPED THE FURTHER EDUCATION SECTOR?

Ideological, economic and social policies continually influence development within FE. The Butler Act (1944) came about following a government review of post-war education and it introduced a tripartite system of secondary education, ie grammar, secondary modern and technical schools. Shortly afterwards, following a further review of education the McNair Report (1944) noted that there were deficiencies in the system of recruiting and training teachers, particularly those involved in teaching FE. Over the next three decades and dependent upon the incumbent government and the political focus, intermittent reviews of FE resulted in further reports (Willis Jackson Report, 1957; Russell Report, 1966) being published, all of which continued to promote the concept of raising the quality of provision in FE by having a qualified workforce. Although at this time it was not mandatory to become qualified, for those that did, the training they received concentrated on skills rather than theoretical development.

Initial Teacher Education

From 1972 FE continued to face significant micro- and macro-political and financial challenges. Teacher training was mostly accredited by awarding bodies (for example, City & Guilds or Edexcel) but the James Report (1972) promoted ITT also being accredited by universities. The teacher training courses offered by universities were often of a higher level than those offered by the awarding bodies.

Twenty years after the James Report, and with an emphasis on a more cost-efficient approach, the government, in 1992, transferred responsibility for funding and governing ITT from local education authorities to FE funding councils. Colleges, managed by a board of governors and senior management, were responsible for their own financial management. However, they still needed to adhere to national strategies that were in force and some colleges failed to meet the '*standards that were acceptable to the Government or funding authorities*' (Tight, 2002, p 139). By 1998 the then Labour government's focus was on education as a means for providing social inclusion and prosperity, and they considered a skilled teaching workforce an essential component towards achieving this.

Further Education National Training Organisation

A Green Paper, entitled *The Learning Age*, commissioned by David Blunkett (1998), recommended the implementation of a further education national training organisation (FENTO) to oversee and endorse teacher training qualifications. In 2001 FENTO rolled out a set of standards to be met through training for a recognised teaching qualification. However, these (and FENTO) failed '*to deliver a professional framework to raise the quality of teaching in further education*' (Lucas, 2004, p 106). FENTO were replaced in 2007 by Lifelong Learning UK (LLUK) who produced another set of standards to replace those of FENTO. These standards contained core units of assessment, within a 120-credit framework; namely:

o   Preparing to Teach in the Lifelong Learning Sector (PTLLS) at level 3 or 4;

o   Certificate in Teaching in the Lifelong Learning Sector (CTLLS) at level 3 or 4;

o   Diploma in Teaching in the Lifelong Learning Sector (DTLLS) at level 5.

Additionally, some higher education institutions (HEIs) offered:

o   Certificate in Education in the Lifelong Learning Sector (Cert.Ed) at level 5 – equivalent to the DTLLS level 5 qualification;

o   Professional Graduate Certificate in Teaching in the Lifelong Learning Sector (PGCE) at level 6;

o   Postgraduate Certificate in Teaching in the Lifelong Learning Sector (PGCE) at level 7.

A PTLLS qualification provided trainee teachers with an initial licence to practise, following which they studied for a CTLLS or DTLLS qualification (or one of the similar qualifications delivered by UK universities). Whether a trainee enrolled onto a CTLLS or a DTLLS ITT qualification was dependent upon their job role and teaching responsibilities as described by the LLUK (2007). CTLLS was seen to be suitable for teachers who did not have a full teaching role. Upon achievement of the CTLLS qualification teachers could apply for Associate Teacher of Learning and Skills (ATLS) status. The DTLLS qualification was seen as suitable for teachers who had a full teaching role. Upon achievement of the DTLLS qualification teachers could apply for Qualified Teacher of Learning and Skills (QTLS) status.

THE AWARD IN EDUCATION AND TRAINING

A review of ITT for the FE sector by Lord Lingfield in 2012 claimed that PTLLS, CTLLS and DTLLS had not had the impact on raising the quality of teaching that had been intended, with not as many teachers as had been anticipated taking up the opportunity to become qualified. Lingfield's final report in the autumn of 2012 concluded that there should no longer be a mandatory requirement to become qualified, although employers still needed to ensure that their staff had the skills to deliver high quality learning. The demise of the LLUK following deregulation and the rise of another body, namely, the Learning Skills Improvement Services (LSIS), provided a further opportunity to '*review, rename and simplify the teaching qualifications*' (LSIS, 2013, p 5). It was from this review that another suite of qualifications emerged; one of these qualifications was the level 3 AET qualification.

The purpose of the AET

The AET qualification is suitable for people who want to pursue a career in teaching, people who already have some involvement in teaching and for assessors who may, for a variety of reasons, want to achieve the AET.

The purpose of the level 3 AET is to provide trainee teachers with an introduction to a range of skills and some underpinning theoretical knowledge that prepares them for working in FE.

According to the RCF, the AET is a level 3 qualification (which has the same level of difficulty but not necessarily the same breadth as A levels). It is the first of a suite of three generic teaching and training qualifications, ie:

○   Award in Education and Training (AET); level 3 – 12 credits;

○   Certificate in Education and Training (CET); level 4 – 30 credits;

○   Diploma in Education and Training (DET); level 5 – 120 credits.

Entry requirements

There are no formal entry requirements for the AET but you will need to have good levels of reading and writing skills in order to prepare for and to write the necessary assignments. It is likely that, at the beginning of your course, your tutor will assess your level of English, mathematics and ICT skills in order for you to be able to draw up a plan of action to support your development in these areas.

Practice requirements

You will be required to engage in a microteaching session for a minimum of one hour during which time you will be assessed on your ability to teach (usually a topic of your choice) for a minimum of 15 minutes. A further 45 minutes can be spent doing more microteaching sessions or by watching others doing their microteaching (Chapter 6 provides further information about microteaching). There is no requirement within the AET for any other observations of your teaching.

The credits that make up the AET

If you look at Figure 1 you will see that the AET can be achieved by studying for, and passing, a variety of units. Some of these are mandatory and some are optional.

Figure 1 Mandatory and optional units for the AET (taken from LSIS, 2013)

Mandatory units level and credits				
Understanding roles, responsibilities and relationships in education and training			Level 3, 3 credits Education and Training unit	
Optional units level and credits			Optional units level and credits	
Understanding and using inclusive learning and teaching approaches in education and training	Level 3, 6 credits Education and Training unit	OR	Facilitating learning and development in groups	Level 3, 6 credits Learning and Development unit
		OR	Facilitating learning and development in individuals	Level 3, 6 credits Learning and Development unit
Understanding assessment in education and training	Level 3, 3 credits Education and Training unit	OR	Understanding the principles and practices of assessment	Level 3, 3 credits Learning and Development unit

The chapters within this book cover the range of topics that are included in all of these units.

THE EDUCATION TRAINING FOUNDATION

All of the units that are situated within the AET are underpinned by the overarching standards outlined by the Education Training Foundation (ETF). The ETF was founded in October 2013, is owned by the FE and Skills sector and is funded by Business Innovation and Skills (BIS) and through commercial finance (ETF, www.et-foundation. co.uk/). At the beginning of this book you will find a table that aligns each chapter to the ETF standards.

SUMMARY OF KEY POINTS

Working within FE provides ongoing opportunities to:

○ develop your own skills and knowledge;

○ develop the skills and knowledge of others (ie your learners);

○ make a difference to the lives of others (ie your learners).

TAKING IT FURTHER

Education & Training Foundation (ETF) (2014) Homepage. [online] Available at: www.et-foundation.co.uk/

The ETF provides up-to-date information about changes to teaching and training in FE.

Excellence Gateway (no date) *Addressing Literacy, Language, Numeracy and ICT Needs in Education and Training: Defining the Minimum Core of Teachers' Knowledge, Understanding and Personal Skills.* [online] Available at: www. excellencegateway.org.uk/content/import-pdf93-0

This site provides a range of information and some resources about the development of the minimum core of teachers' knowledge, understanding and personal skills.

REFERENCES

Blunkett, D (1998) *The Learning Age.* Green Paper: Response Summary. [online] Available at: http://www.leeds.ac.uk/educol/documents/summary.pdf (accessed November 2015).

Butler Act (1944) *The Cabinet Papers 1915–1986.* The National Archives. [online] Available at: http://www.nationalarchives.gov.uk/cabinetpapers/ (accessed November 2015).

Department for Business, Innovation and Skills (BIS) (no date) Homepage [online] Available at: www.gov.uk/government/organisations/department-for-business-innovation-skills (accessed January 2016).

Department for Education and Skills (DfES) (2004) *Equipping Our Teachers for the Future.* London: DfES.

Department of Education and Science (1972) *The James Report: Teacher Education and Training.* London: Her Majesty's Stationery Office.

Learning Skills Improvement Services (LSIS) (2013) *Teaching and Training Qualifications for the Further Education and Skills Sector in England: Guidance for Employees and Practitioners.* Coventry: LSIS. [online] Available at: http://repository.excellencegateway. org.uk/fedora/objects/eg:6626/datastreams/DOC/content (accessed September 2014).

Lifelong Learning UK (LLUK) (2007) *New Overarching Professional Standards for Teachers, Trainers and Tutors.* London: LLUK.

Lingfield, R (2012) *Professionalism in Further Education: Final Report.* London: Department for Business, Innovation and Skills.

Lucas, N (2004) The FENTO Fandango: National Standards, Compulsory Teaching Qualifications and the Growing Regulation of FE College Teachers. *Journal of Further and Higher Education*, 28(1): 35–51.

McNair Report (1944) *Report of the Committee Appointed by the President of the Board of Education to Consider the Supply, Recruitment and Training of Teachers and Youth Leaders*. London: HMSO.

Russell Report (1966) *The Supply and Training of Teachers for Further Education*. London: Department of Education and Science.

Skills Commission (2009) *Skills Commission into Teacher Training in Vocational Education*. London: Skills Commission.

Tight, M (2002) *Key Concepts in Adult Education and Training*. Abingdon: Routledge.

Willis Jackson Report (1957) *The Supply and Training of Teachers in Technical Colleges*. London: HMSO.

1 Understanding roles, responsibilities and relationships

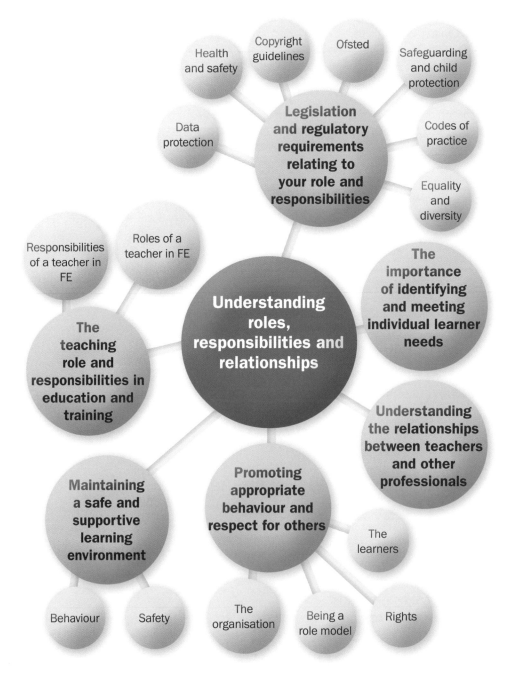

INTRODUCTION

As a teacher in FE you will have a variety of roles and responsibilities. Many of them will be the same as those of other teachers who are employed in your organisation or in other FE organisations. However, some may apply specifically to your area of work and/or your contract of employment. Some variance in roles and responsibilities is due to the diversity of the students who enrol in the range of courses that are offered in the FE sector as well as the different types of training and learning organisations in which they are delivered. For example, you could be teaching a group of 14-year-old students who are working towards a qualification that will enhance their employment opportunities (for example, construction, accountancy) or you could be teaching a group of adults who have enrolled on a vocational course in order to pursue a hobby (for example, creative writing, languages). This chapter develops your knowledge of your role and responsibilities as a teacher and how these, along with the policies that guide these, are implemented.

OBJECTIVES

This chapter covers the learning outcomes of the following AET mandatory units (Group A, learning outcomes 1–3, level 3, 3 credits):

1   Understand the teaching role and responsibilities in education and training.

2   Understand ways to maintain a safe and supportive learning environment.

3   Understand the relationships between teachers and other professionals in education and training.

The chapter therefore develops your understanding of the following:

- o   the teaching role and responsibilities in education and training;
- o   key aspects of legislation, regulatory requirements and codes of practice;
- o   equality and diversity;
- o   maintaining a safe and supportive learning environment;
- o   identification of individual learner needs;
- o   working with other professionals;
- o   behaviour management;
- o   role boundaries;
- o   referrals to meet individual needs.

See Table 1 at the front of the book for how this chapter covers aspects of the ETF (2014) standards.

STARTING POINT

o   What do you expect your roles to be as a teacher?

o   What responsibilities do you expect to have?

THE TEACHING ROLE AND RESPONSIBILITIES IN EDUCATION AND TRAINING

Although your roles and responsibilities in FE will vary and will depend on any agreement made at the commencement of your employment, there will be many similarities and mandatory requirements whether you are employed full or part time, teaching in a college or other type of FE organisation or teaching on academic or vocational awards.

Roles of a teacher in FE

As a teacher your role will be multifaceted. You need to make the learning enjoyable (this aids motivation) while also enabling all of your learners to develop their knowledge and skills. You will use a variety of strategies to do this which will include some teacher-led (didactic) teaching but this should be kept to a minimum and most strategies will be student-led (eg group work, research). A student-led approach to teaching helps learners to take some responsibility for their own learning.

As a teacher it is important that you:

o   understand the scheme/schedule of work;

o   understand the assessment criteria;

o   design programmes of study;

o   carry out initial assessments;

o   communicate clearly to others;

o   provide a safe learning environment;

o   promote appropriate behaviour for learning;

o   manage the groups and their learning;

o   promote inclusion;

o   be knowledgeable in the subject;

o   know how to gain additional support for you and your learners;

o   be organised;

o   carry out summative and formative assessments;

o   provide appropriate feedback;

○   keep records of progress;

○   monitor attendance and punctuality;

○   enter learners for examinations.

Responsibilities of a teacher in FE

As a teacher your responsibilities will include:

○   adhering to policy and legislation;

○   applying policy and legislation;

○   ensuring you complete your own continual professional development so that you stay up to date;

○   setting and maintaining high standards;

○   collaborating with others in the team;

○   being dependable, trustworthy and conscientious;

○   abiding by any codes of conduct applicable to your sector;

○   doing a good job such as differentiating and personalising the learning to meet individual needs;

○   keeping accurate records;

○   knowing who to refer your learners to for additional support such as in relation to finance.

LEGISLATION AND REGULATORY REQUIREMENTS RELATING TO YOUR ROLE AND RESPONSIBILITIES

It is the responsibility of the organisation to ensure that you have relevant up-to-date training in relation to appropriate legislation and your job roles and responsibilities. It is, of course, your responsibility to make sure that you attend and/or take the appropriate action to take up the training offered. There is some legislation that will be applicable to all teachers while others will be applicable or more relevant to certain disciplines or sectors. Organisations will have policies in place regarding much of this and will also have a named point of contact. Make sure you adhere to any specific policies or laws relating to your area and ask your line manager or one of your peers if you are unsure. At the beginning of your employment your organisation may arrange an induction (familiarisation) process for you; it is your responsibility to ask for clarification if there is some procedure and/or area of legislation which you are not quite sure about.

Activity

Think about what roles and responsibilities you might have as a teacher. Keep these in mind as you read through the rest of this chapter and this book.

Equality and diversity

Up until 2010 any legislation relating to equality, for example race, sex and disability dis-crimination, was located in individual Acts and reports. Since 2010 all Acts and reports relating to equality can be found within the Equality Act (2010). Within this one Act are several key protected characteristics that are considered significant in order to help to protect individuals from harassment, discrimination or victimisation. These relate to:

o   age;

o   disability;

o   pregnancy or maternity;

o   gender reassignment;

o   race;

o   religion or belief;

o   gender;

o   sexual orientation.

Much of this legislation is about helping to protect people's human rights. You will also find more specific legislation regarding this in the Human Rights Act (1998). The Equality Act (2010) applies not only to people but also to where they work. For example, organisa-tions need to make sure that their workplace is accessible to all stakeholders and they are expected to make reasonable adjustments, as required, to the premises. More information can be obtained from the Equality and Human Rights Commission (EHRC) (2015).

Activity

Do you know what is meant by harassment, discrimination and victimisation?

Comment

According to the EHRC (2015):

o   **harassment** means unwanted behaviour that affects someone's dignity or creates an unpleasant environment;

o   **discrimination** means treating someone unfairly;

o   **victimisation** is when someone is treated less favourably because they have, or are believed to have, made a complaint, claim or allegation relating to the Act against someone else or helped someone to do this.

The Human Rights Act (1998) covers the rights and freedoms that belong to all people and apply to all members of a fair society. Some of the rights are absolute such as the right of protection from torture while others are limited such as the right to liberty. Some are called qualified rights where the rights of an individual have to be weighed against the needs of society. Equality sits within the Human Rights Act, as does the right to an education.

Activity

Why do you think education is a qualified right?

Comment

Education is a qualified right because although all children are entitled to education they could be denied access to education that the state considered inappropriate.

Data protection

The Data Protection Act (1998) ensures that organisations store any information that they keep about teachers and learners safely. It is your responsibility to ensure that information that you collect is stored securely, is only passed to the relevant people and not shared with others. You must also ensure that you use the information appropriately and not for any other purpose than that for which it was intended when collected. You will have access to a wide range of data (for example, learners' details) and you must think carefully who you share this with.

Health and safety

All training providers must provide a safe learning environment. Of particular importance is the Health and Safety at Work Act (1974), which is the key legislation aimed at keeping you and your learners safe. There have been numerous amendments when the government have become aware of potential hazards within the workplace. If you have any questions make sure that you find out who the designated health and safety representative is and speak with them. If you do have concerns regarding health and safety it is your responsibility to report them either to your line manager or to the designated health and safety representative. Always check organisational policy so you are aware of what relates to you and your students.

Safeguarding and child protection

Child protection comes under the wider umbrella of Safeguarding. Child protection takes two main forms. Firstly, under section 17 of the Children Act (1989) are children 'in need', who are vulnerable because their health or development is likely to be impaired if they do not gain access to additional services. Secondly, under section 47 of the Children Act (1989) are children who are at risk from physical, sexual, or emotional abuse or neglect. Both parts of this legislation are about making sure that children are protected from harm but this legislation can also be applied to vulnerable adults. If you have contact with young and/or vulnerable adults and suspect that any of them are in danger of abuse of any kind then you should speak to the designated safeguarding lead (DSL) at your workplace.

Under the Safeguarding policy you are required to complete a Disclosure and Barring Service (DBS) check if you are likely to come into contact with children and/or vulnerable adults. In addition, who you live with may bar you from successfully gaining your DBS check and honesty is important. Under the Children Act (2004), children are identified as anyone under the age of 18 so you can see some learners in an FE college will still be classed as children in the eyes of the law.

In the current climate, schools, colleges and training establishments are required to consider the 'Prevent Duty', which is outlined in the Counter-Terrorism and Security Act (2015). This is about the responsibilities educational settings have to prevent children and young people from being drawn into terrorism. The Prevent Duty is not about pre-venting children and young people from having controversial political and religious views but about encouraging them to operate within the law and proceed without developing extremism. Schools and colleges are encouraged to reduce the chances of radicalisa-tion by promoting 'British values' which include valuing democracy, the law, individual liberty, and mutual respect and tolerance of those with different faiths and beliefs.

Codes of practice

Many organisations have their own codes of practice that employees must adhere to; for example, codes of practice for healthcare workers, police officers, support workers, assessors and, of course, teachers. Most codes of practice focus on ensuring employees are professional and show qualities such as integrity and honesty. There are professional standards for teachers and trainers in the FE sector in England which were updated in 2014 and have been devised by the ETF. See the introduction for further information.

Copyright guidelines

There are guidelines in relation to copying materials, which means that you must acknowledge the source of material for any handouts and lecture material that you use. In addition, you need to follow the guidance relating to how much material you can pho-tocopy from books. You will usually find advice regarding this near the photocopier, often pinned on the wall. At larger organisations there is likely to be a department responsible for reproducing material and they would easily be able to give you additional advice. Scanning chapters from books and putting them onto your organisation's Virtual Learning Environment (VLE) should be avoided unless you have gained permission to do so.

Ofsted

Ofsted is responsible for ensuring educational provision is of a good or excellent standard. The FE sector is inspected regularly to assure the quality of provision. The frequency of inspection depends on the grade given at the last inspection. The grades that an organisa-tion could receive are outstanding, good, requires improvement and inadequate.

As well as being quality assured by Ofsted your organisation will also have some system for measuring performance such as annual lesson observations. Increasingly the observation process is part of a broader process which gathers evidence of your practice. Learner surveys, learner attendance and attainment are often part of this process. This data is saved and as well as being used for organisational purposes as required is also given to Ofsted during inspections. Ofsted not only look at teaching and learning but currently under the revised guidelines for 2015 (Ofsted, 2015) examine things like the leadership of the setting, behaviour management and the general safeguarding arrangements that are in place as well as the steps being taken to prevent extremism and radicalisation.

Activity

o   Read the latest Ofsted report relating to your organisation.

o   Do you know what the organisation is doing to maintain or improve its grade?

Ways to promote equality and value diversity

It is important to promote equality of opportunity as well as valuing the diversity of your learners.

Activity

What do you think equality and diversity mean?

Comment

Equality means ensuring every individual has an equal opportunity to participate and make the most of the opportunities presented to them. People should not be discriminated against because of characteristics such as gender, disability and race.

Diversity means valuing the differences between people and the ways in which those differences can contribute to a richer, more creative and more productive working environment.

So, in your classes you need to make sure that you treat all learners fairly and give everyone the same chances to participate and you should encourage your learners to do the same for each other.

The organisation should have a policy to explain their expectations of staff and learners in relation to equality and diversity and it is up to you to convey this to your learners through your behaviour as a teacher; in this capacity you need to be a positive role model. You also need to consider equality and diversity in the materials you produce, so ensure your learning resources are free from prejudice and represent people from all walks of life. One of your roles as a teacher is to challenge any unacceptable comments from your learners which they may make because of ignorance or prejudice. What is acceptable and unacceptable behaviour is covered in more detail later in this chapter.

You might want to think about the following ideas to address issues of equality and diversity:

o   handouts: consider the colour of the paper and the font size and type (use a sans serif font for clarity); make sure that they are suitable for all your learners (do any learners have dyslexia or are any visually impaired?). Make sure that any illustrations that you use avoid any bias. Try and produce some of your handouts in a format that can easily be adapted by learners to suit their needs or preferences;

o   language: use neutral language such as *wipe board, they, police officer,* avoid jargon, explain technical language clearly, and provide a glossary;

o   visual displays: consider the font size, font style and background colour (some learners with dyslexia find it difficult to read fonts on white backgrounds so consider using pale yellow or blue, for example);

o   learning environment: adjust the lighting as appropriate, open a window if necessary, avoid clutter;

o   Virtual Learning Environment (VLE): ask your line manager about the organisational policy of uploading materials onto the VLE. Some organisations expect teachers to upload materials before each class so that learners can print in the font they prefer or on the colour they prefer.

 Case study

You are undertaking one-to-one tutorials with your English evening class. One of your learners tells you that they think they have dyslexia. Their brother was diagnosed in secondary school and they have the same issues with reading and writing as he does.

Activity

What should you do in this case?

Comment

You should get some more information about the issues that they are having. You should also refer them, if possible, to an expert in dyslexia who will test them to see if they have dyslexia or not. You could also ask the learner if using a different coloured background on the resources provided would help. You could also ask if they wanted to have the resources you use for each lesson in advance so they have the opportunity to pre-read them. The learner has potentially been coping for a long time with the issues that they have, so while you are waiting for the recommendations to come back from the assessment, ask if they have any existing strategies.

THE IMPORTANCE OF IDENTIFYING AND MEETING INDIVIDUAL LEARNER NEEDS

Equality is often the driver behind meeting individual needs, and learners with Special Educational Needs and Disabilities (SEND) are likely to have additional needs. You must make sure that you are aware of these needs and cater for these within the constraints of the organisation and the law. Check if there are any learning support agreements for learners in your classes if you take over an existing group. You also need to make sure that any assessment methods used are appropriate and that praise and encouragement are given to all learners.

As part of the initial assessments in your organisation you should be able to identify if learners may have an additional learning need as well as a preferred learning style, although you need to provide a varied learning environment that will cater for (and challenge) all learners. Doing an initial assessment will help you to decide if any learners need any further assessment in order to develop a specific education plan for them. Once these initial and any additional assessments have been completed you will be more informed to decide what adjustments you need to make for any specific learner so that they are not disadvantaged in any teaching and learning situation. Some learners may be eligible for support in or out of class so make sure that you liaise with any support workers to find out what it is you need to do to ensure that they can best support the learner(s) allocated to them. You might, for instance, need to send a scheme of work, a lesson plan or resources prior to a teaching and learning session.

MAINTAINING A SAFE AND SUPPORTIVE LEARNING ENVIRONMENT

Organisations are required to ensure a safe learning environment. The rooms must be free from hazards and all electrical equipment must be tested regularly and meet safety standards. You should report anything you see that you feel is causing a hazard or looks to be dangerous. In addition, at the start of any course or training you need to make sure you share safety information with the learners, for example where the nearest emergency exits are, and who is a first aider and where to find them.

> ### Activity
>
> Do you know who is responsible for health and safety and first aid in your organisation?

In order to create a safe learning environment you also need to consider how you and the learners interact to make it emotionally safe as well. This can be a complicated area and it is worth remembering that what works well for one group may not work for others. In addition, what works for one teacher may not work for another and what works in one subject may not be appropriate for another either. It is also a teacher's responsibility to protect learners' emotional needs and protect learners against any harassment.

Behaviour

As a teacher it is important that you recognise what is and is not acceptable behaviour. Your organisation should have a behaviour policy and it is worth looking at this to make sure you follow the guidelines and know what to do if something is not right. In addition, it is a good idea to discuss with your learners at the beginning of any new course what is acceptable in your classroom and what is not. These rules may be dictated by the organisation or you may need to draw up your own. You could encourage the learners to design the class rules and then consider getting them to put these rules in an agreement which they all sign. If possible, display this in the classroom.

Safety

As well as being a legislative requirement, you do, of course, want your learners to be safe so make sure you follow safeguarding procedures when applicable and make sure you know who to go to. Particularly, if your classes are scheduled in an evening or at a weekend when the organisation may have fewer staff make sure you know who to contact should any issue arise. Generally, look out for suspicious behaviour from people in the buildings and immediately report anything that you consider unusual or suspicious. Also make sure you handle any equipment safely as per manufacturers' guidelines and the organisation's health and safety policy. Importantly, if you do extra-curricular activities, for example an outdoor activity or trip, make sure you adhere to the organisation's risk assessment procedure.

PROMOTING APPROPRIATE BEHAVIOUR AND RESPECT FOR OTHERS

Being a role model

As a professional you need to be a good role model to your learners. You need to wear suitable clothing for the job and to look professional. You need to make sure you use the right terminology and the right language so that you do not cause offence and you should not swear. As a teacher you should be enthusiastic, arrive at your teaching and learning sessions on time and be organised. If you do this you can not only expect but can request the same from your learners.

The organisation

As already mentioned, the organisation will have a behaviour policy and it is a good idea to discuss this with the learners and also to ask them to agree to acceptable standards of behaviour. Learners do need to be aware of acceptable behaviour and the consequences of not adhering to these accepted standards of behaviour.

The learners

Watch out for bullying. It is not just something that happens with younger learners; it can happen with adults. Bullies can be either learners or staff. Bullying comes within the Safeguarding policy and is classed as unacceptable behaviour. As the teacher you must watch for interactions between learners and challenge anything you see that goes against the law, policy or common sense. Bullying can be verbal as well as physical so hover, listen and intervene if needed; this ensures the learners remain on task too.

Remember that adults in group work and class work are more likely to exhibit challenging behaviour rather than be 'bad', so make sure that learners are clear on what you and the organisation see as inappropriate behaviour and how it will be dealt with. Be aware too about how alleged jokes are perceived. It may not have been the intention to cause upset but that may have been the outcome. Bullying and its consequences should be considered when you and the learners are setting ground rules at the beginning of the course.

Rights

When you start to work you should be given a contract to sign and it is important that you read it carefully before you sign it.

If you are not already, you might want to consider being a member of a union, as they advise and help their members with policy and legal rights. There are several related to the sector such as the University and College Union (UCU) or the Association of Teachers and Lecturers (ATL). The rates to join vary depending on whether you are full time or part time. A union can advise you and help to protect your rights. You should have a representative at your organisation and you may want to check who this is before joining. The local area will have area representatives too.

 Case study

Julie is a quiet young teacher at the FE college and works in catering. You teach health and social care and work in a different department. One day you find her upset in the staff room where she tells you that her head of department, Greg, had just blocked her exit from the stock cupboard off the teaching kitchen making it awkward for her to escape, while he made suggestive comments to her. It turns out he has been doing this for a while. She tells you she hates coming to work.

Activity

What, if anything, might you do?

Answer

This is not acceptable behaviour from anyone, let alone her head of department, and this kind of bullying behaviour should not go on. The best way to deal with it is to find out what Julie wants but it is probable that she just wants it to stop. He may intend it as a joke, which is no excuse, but helps explain why you should try to deal with something like this at the lowest level first. She could consider some of the following options:

- o   tell him to stop in person or by letter/email;

- o   be accompanied by her friend/union rep and tell him to stop;

- o   ask you or someone else to speak to him;

- o   report it officially to the Equality Representative so that it is dealt with more officially.

UNDERSTANDING THE RELATIONSHIPS BETWEEN TEACHERS AND OTHER PROFESSIONALS

Although at times you may feel that you are working in isolation, that is not the case and the bigger the organisation the more people you will get involved with in order to do your job. There is nothing wrong with becoming friends with people you work with but it is important that you remain professional. It is also best to remain professional at all times with learners but in small communities this can be difficult, so make sure you do nothing that will compromise yourself as a teacher.

Activity

Make a list of all the people with whom you will need to communicate in your role as a teacher.

You are primarily a teacher and employed to do that role. At times learners may share inappropriate or confidential information and it is important to realise what you can deal with yourself and what you need to refer to other people inside or outside your organisation. You want your learners to achieve their best and to do this they may need help from others. Sometimes it is your role to refer them to others who are able to help and have earned the qualifications to do so. Your learners may wish you to treat what they tell you confidentially; however, it is worth remembering that you may have a legal responsibility to pass on this information to someone else. You need to know who the relevant people are to help learners (from inside and outside of your organisation). In a larger organisation there should be people who can provide support in the following areas:

- o financial support;

- o counselling;

- o careers advice;

- o additional learning support;

- o academic skills support;

- o personal tutoring;

- o learning resource support;

- o IT support;

- o safeguarding.

Activity

- o Do you know who, if anyone, covers the above roles in your organisation?

- o In some cases you may need to refer learners to outside agencies. Can you think of some examples where this might be necessary?

You may need to refer learners to one of the numerous organisations outside your organisation that are staffed by trained people who may be able to offer help, sometimes all night long. Such organisations include:

- o Citizens Advice Bureau who can offer wide-ranging advice;

- o Samaritans who offer 24-hour emotional support;

- o National Debt line who give free advice on debt issues;

- o Shelter who are a charity advising about housing and homelessness;

- o Victim Support who advise victims of crime.

Activity

A learner comes to you to discuss the following problems. Who would you refer them to if you felt it did not come under your role? Complete the table.

Issue	Who could help?
A learner is having problems with using apostrophes	
A young learner tells you they are being abused by one of their parents	
A learner wants some ideas of job prospects relating to this qualification	
A learner is living in rented accommodation and thinks they may soon be homeless	

Issue	Who could help?
A learner is being subjected to harassment by another learner	
A learner is struggling to understand a concept you delivered last week	
A learner is feeling very stressed at the moment	

SUMMARY OF KEY POINTS

As you become more experienced and settled into your organisation your roles and responsibilities will become second nature. Remember though to:

○ read your contract of employment carefully as this will outline specific and general duties;

○ adhere to all legislation associated with your role as a teacher;

○ promote a positive learning environment at all times;

○ promote positive behaviour at all times;

○ ask your line manager or a colleague if you are unsure about anything.

 Check your understanding

1   Name three roles that you may have as a teacher.

2   Name three responsibilities that you may have as a teacher.

3   List at least three Acts that teachers need to consider.

4   What support mechanisms might you need to access on behalf of your learners?

5   Outline three key points that you have learned through reading this chapter.

 TAKING IT FURTHER

Education & Training Foundation (ETF) (2014) *Professional Standards for Teachers and Trainers in Education and Training England.* [online] Available at: www. et-foundation.co.uk/supporting/support-practitioners/professional-standards/

This site provides the ETF standards in full as well as information about events and research in the FE sector.

Machin, L, Hindmarch, D, Murray, S and Richardson, T (2015) *A Complete Guide to the Level 4 Certificate in Education and Training.* 2nd ed. Northwich: Critical Publishing Ltd.

This book provides further information about the key topics covered at level 3 and, through its coverage of the learning outcomes for the CET qualification, can support your development at level 4.

Ministry of Justice (2006) *Making Sense of Human Rights.* [online] Available at: www.justice.gov.uk/downloads/human-rights/human-rights-making-sense-human-rights.pdf

This document explains the information contained in the Human Rights Act, particularly in relation to public safety.

REFERENCES

Education & Training Foundation (ETF) (2014) *Professional Standards for Teachers and Trainers in Education and Training – England.* [online] Available at: www.et-foundation.co.uk/wp-content/uploads/2014/05/4991-Prof-standards-A4_4-2.pdf (accessed 19 February 2016).

Equality and Human Rights Commission (2015) *Key Concepts.* [online] Available at: www.equalityhumanrights.com/private-and-public-sector-guidance/education-providers/schools-guidance/key-concepts (accessed 9 November 2015).

Ofsted (2015) *School Inspection Handbook from September 2015.* [online] Available at: www.gov.uk/government/publications/school-inspection-handbook-from-september-2015 (accessed 9 November 2015).

The Children Act (1989). [online] Available at: www.legislation.gov.uk/ukpga/1989/41/contents (accessed 9 November 2015).

The Children Act (2004). [online] Available at: www.legislation.gov.uk/ukpga/2004/31/contents (accessed 9 November 2015).

The Counter-Terrorism and Security Act (2015). [online] Available at: www.legislation.gov.uk/ukpga/2015/6/contents (accessed 9 November 2015).

The Data Protection Act (1998). [online] Available at: www.legislation.gov.uk/ukpga/1998/29/contents (accessed 9 November 2015).

The Equality Act (2010). [online] Available at: www.legislation.gov.uk/ukpga/2010/15/contents (accessed 9 November 2015).

The Health and Safety at Work Act (1974). [online] Available at: www.legislation.gov.uk/ukpga/1974/37/contents (accessed 9 November 2015).

The Human Rights Act (1998). [online] Available at: www.legislation.gov.uk/ukpga/1998/42/contents (accessed 9 November 2015).

2 Understanding inclusive teaching and learning

What is inclusive teaching and learning?

Understanding inclusive teaching and learning

Ways to establish ground rules with learners

Why is inclusive teaching and learning important?

Ways to engage and motivate learners

Teaching and learning approaches

Creating an inclusive teaching and learning environment

Developing learners' wider skills

Learning domains

Resources

Additional support

INTRODUCTION

This chapter develops your understanding of inclusive teaching and learning. This will help you to implement inclusive teaching and learning into your everyday practice.

OBJECTIVES

This chapter covers the learning outcomes of the following AET optional units (Group B, learning outcomes 1–2, level 3, 6 credits):

- Understanding and using inclusive teaching and learning approaches in education and training (Education and Training unit).

The chapter therefore develops your understanding of the following:

- how to create an inclusive teaching and learning environment;
- the strengths and limitations of teaching and learning approaches used in your area of specialism in relation to meeting individual learner needs;
- how to provide opportunities for learners to develop their English, mathematics, ICT and wider skills;
- ways to engage and motivate learners;
- ways to establish ground rules with learners.

See *Table 1 at the front of the book for how this chapter covers aspects of the ETF (2014) standards.*

STARTING POINT

What do you already know about inclusive teaching and learning?

- Do you know what inclusive teaching and learning means?
- Do you know why inclusive teaching and learning is important?

WHAT IS INCLUSIVE TEACHING AND LEARNING?

Inclusive teaching and learning is the approach taken when you use strategies that ensure all of your learners, whatever their differences, are supported and engaged in lessons. Inclusive teaching and recognising that every learner is different will underpin all that you do as a teacher and requires that you treat learners as individuals, taking into consideration their specific needs, preferences, backgrounds and behaviours.

Activity

Think about your past learning experiences. Have there been any instances when you or others in your class weren't actively included in the lesson?

Comment

When answering the question above you may have drawn on experiences from school, college or university of when you, or others, felt excluded rather than included in the learning environment. Examples of actions that can detract from an inclusive learning environment include:

o   a teacher who brushed over topics that you didn't understand;

o   a teacher who allowed learners to work in friendship groups to the exclusion of others or who appeared to have favourites;

o   occasions in which negative stereotypes were used or left unchallenged;

o   an occasion in which a wheelchair user or a learner with a disability or learning difficulty had reduced access to school facilities and resources.

WHY IS INCLUSIVE TEACHING AND LEARNING IMPORTANT?

Activity

Why do you think that inclusive teaching and learning approaches are important?

Comment

Inclusive teaching and learning is important, not only because it meets legal and quality assurance (Ofsted) requirements, but also because it benefits a range of interested parties including learners, teachers and teaching organisations.

Benefits to learners:

o   learners feel motivated, engaged and part of a larger community;

o   a positive environment is created in which all feel valued and listened to.

Benefits to teachers:

o   the classroom environment becomes more positive, and easier to manage;

o   teaching is more enjoyable;

o   you form more positive relationships with learners.

Benefits to the institution:

o   requirements are met in terms of a range of legislation in relation to inclusivity, including the Equality Act (2010).

CREATING AN INCLUSIVE TEACHING AND LEARNING ENVIRONMENT

In order to create an optimum teaching and learning environment you will need to have an awareness of your learners in terms of their differences, similarities and specific needs.

Activity

In what ways do you think learners may differ?

Comment

Learners differ in endless ways, though some key differences can be considered in terms of age, disability or learning difficulty, social background, culture, gender, race, sexual orientation, family and personal commitments. All of these differences contribute to learners' individualisation and should be welcomed within the classroom as they can contribute to an engaging and positive learning environment.

Additional support

In order to provide an inclusive learning environment, it may (as noted in Chapter 1) sometimes be necessary for you to seek additional support for one or more of your learners. Examples of additional support include:

o   counselling;

o   financial support;

o   student clubs and societies;

o   study support;

o   additional learning support;

o   assistive technology for learners with disabilities.

Resources

Organisational or external support is essential in providing an inclusive learning environment, but equally essential is the support that you, as a teacher, offer in the classroom. One way to do this is through resources, as Table 2.1 shows.

Table 2.1 Resources to support inclusivity

Resource	Who benefits?
Large print handouts	Learners with visual impairment
Images combined with text in handouts	All learners – handouts become easier to read and digest
Coloured overlays or coloured paper	Learners with dyslexia
Supplementary handouts	Learners of varying abilities
Stepped handouts of increasing difficulty	Learners of varying abilities
Glossary of key terms	All learners
Provide a range of different resources	All learners, whatever their learning preference

Learners also differ in terms of their learning preferences. For example, in terms of learning something new, some learners will prefer lectures, some will prefer hands-on activities, while others will prefer reading.

One way in which these learning preferences can be categorised is in terms of learning styles, with learners being categorised as Visual, Auditory or Kinaesthetic (often called VAK) learners; see Table 2.2. A number of learning style questionnaires are available that you might want to use to determine the learning preference(s) of your learners.

Table 2.2 Learning styles

Learning style	Comment
Visual	• Visual learners have a preference for images, mind maps and visual tools • May prefer visual notes for a lecture, engaging with handouts or creating posters
Auditory	• Auditory learners have a preference for with hearing information • May prefer lectures, audio recordings or discussions
Kinaesthetic	• Kinaesthetic learners thrive on physical experiences • They may learn by engaging in presentations, role play or a range of activities that get them out of their seats

While not an exact science, learning styles are one way in which you can review the variety of teaching methods that you can use to create an inclusive learning environment.

TEACHING AND LEARNING APPROACHES

Teaching is much more than the imparting of knowledge from one person to others; in reality it is a little more complicated. Teaching does involve the teaching of knowledge; however, it also involves teaching practical and academic skills and attitudes.

Learning domains: teaching of knowledge, skills and attitudes

Knowledge, skills and attitudes can each be linked to a specific learning domain or type of learning, with the cognitive domain referring to the teaching of knowledge (Bloom, 1956), the psychomotor domain (Simpson, 1966) referring to the teaching of practical skills and the affective domain (Krathwohl et al, 1964) referring to the teaching of attitudes.

Table 2.3 gives some examples of teaching methods that can be used for each of the domains, though the list is not exhaustive.

Table 2.3 Learning domains

Learning domain	Examples	Teaching methods
Cognitive domain	Memorising historical dates	Lecture
	Evaluating a chapter in a book	Quiz
		Gapped handouts
Affective domain	Attitudes to equality and diversity	Discussion
		Debates
	Adhering to classroom rules	Role play
Psychomotor domain	Playing a sport	Demonstration
	Painting a picture	Simulation

Whatever subject you teach you will be teaching elements within each of the learning domains. For example, if you were teaching learners to paint a picture you would use teaching methods that enabled them to develop the necessary skills to paint but you would also need to use teaching methods that developed learners' knowledge in terms of colour combinations, paint types and what brushes are the most appropriate for a given task.

As a teacher, your choice of teaching methods will be up to you. When you are making this decision you should draw on your knowledge of your learners in order to ensure that your methods are inclusive, with all learners being actively engaged in the lesson. A common mistake that new teachers make is to plan their lessons around methods that they themselves would prefer as learners, whereas what is usually required is a variety of methods that will create a balanced lesson.

> ### Activity
>
> You will need to match your teaching methods to other organisational factors such as room size, layout, resources, location and even group size. Why do you think this is important?

A range of factors can change the effectiveness of your teaching method; for example, a teaching method that works well with a small group of learners may be ineffective with a larger group. For this reason, when considering methods to use, you should consider the strengths and limitations of each. Table 2.4 explores this in more detail.

Table 2.4 Strengths and limitations of teaching methods

Teaching method	Strengths	Limitations
Lecture	Can be good way of imparting a large amount of information to learners Good for auditory learners	Learners can lose focus if the lecture is too long
Quiz	Can be a fun way of engaging the learners with a little healthy competition	Can be perceived as a test Need to consider impact on less confident learners
Gapped handouts	Learners can work at their own pace Teacher can focus support on learners who are struggling	Can take time to create Need to ensure high quality May be perceived as 'easy' by some
Discussion	An engaging way to draw on learners' knowledge and views	More vocal learners may dominate
Debates	A good way of engaging learners Learners develop verbal skills	Requires skilful classroom management
Role play	Good for developing confidence and interpersonal skills	Not liked by all learners
Demonstration	Effective for smaller group sizes Good for teaching skills	Not so good for larger groups unless enhanced by technology Some aspects of demonstration may be difficult to see

Developing learners' skills: English, mathematics, ICT and wider skills

Table 2.4 notes the strengths and limitations of teaching and learning methods and considers how each can be used to develop learners' wider skills. Wider skills encompass areas such as employability and development of learners' Functional Skills in areas of mathematics, English and ICT. The importance of these skills was noted in the Leitch

Review (2006), which recognised the need for learners (and adults in general) to develop their skills in literacy and numeracy.

The development of these wider skills will aid your learners when seeking employment and within society as a whole. These skills, in addition to subject-specific skills and knowledge, form an important element of what is expected of teachers in the FE sector.

In order to support your learners in developing wider skills you will be expected to incorporate (or embed) them into lessons. By doing this, learners continue to develop in their specialist area while simultaneously developing the essential wider skills that they will need beyond the classroom.

Activity

How might the following wider skills be embedded into a health and safety lesson?

o communication;

o using a computer spreadsheet to create graphs;

o working with percentages;

o letter writing;

o using publishing software.

A range of skills can easily be embedded into lessons in a variety of ways (see Table 2.5). With a little thought, wider skills can be embedded with particular relevance to the learners and their course.

Table 2.5 Embedding wider skills

Wider skill	Learner activity
Communication	• Presenting findings to the group
	• Working collaboratively in small groups
Using a computer spreadsheet to create graphs	• Learners create a graph based on the number of workplace accidents and how they are caused
Working with percentages	• Calculating percentage increases or decreases in accidents over a period of time
Letter writing	• Writing a letter of complaint following a near miss incident in a supermarket
Using publishing software	• Creating a poster warning of workplace hazards

WAYS TO ENGAGE AND MOTIVATE LEARNERS

Motivation is what drives us to do something. We can be driven by external factors, such as a new job, a pay rise or a qualification. We can also be driven by internal factors, such as the enjoyment of doing something or the sense of satisfaction that comes with achievement.

An essential part of creating an inclusive learning environment is engaging and motivating learners. Your choice of a range of engaging teaching and learning approaches is one way in which you can do this; however, your general approach to teaching is also equally important. You should make efforts to form positive relationships with learners, be approachable and supportive and use praise to recognise learner contributions.

Learners may arrive in the classroom tired, reluctant to engage or uninterested in the topic you have planned for them. It is your role as a teacher to find ways to overcome this. This might be through the use of incentives (perhaps an early break or less work to do for homework if work is completed in the class), or how you plan the lesson in order to make it interesting and engaging.

Activity

What approach can you take to teach a topic such as health and safety legislation that might make the lesson more interesting and engaging?

The key to teaching topics that learners may find difficult or which they are unwilling to engage with is to consider the use of innovative teaching and learning methods. Examples include:

○   asking learners to write a song or a poem summarising key points of the legislation;

○   asking learners to act out a scenario where health and safety legislation was not adhered to;

○   asking learners to create a poster, either on the computer or on paper.

WAYS TO ESTABLISH GROUND RULES WITH LEARNERS

Negative classroom behaviour can severely impact on an inclusive learning environment; therefore, you should look to find ways to create an environment where behaviour is positive. This can be done via the use of ground rules, which are expectations of classroom behaviour.

In the past, and perhaps in your own experience, ground rules were imposed on learners, with a statement of what you should or shouldn't do in the classroom. However, the approach taken in the FE sector is not based on imposing rules. Instead, rules are negotiated with the learners, with them having an input and agreeing to the rules.

Most importantly, ground rules should be framed in a positive way. For example, instead of a rule stating 'no shouting out' you might instead word it as 'raise your hand to speak' or 'be respectful of others' views'.

Activity

Why do you think that negotiating rules is the preferred approach in the FE sector?

There are a number of reasons why negotiating rules is the preferred approach for setting rules with learners in the FE sector.

○ Learners are aged from 14+ to mature learners and are more responsive to rules that they have discussed and helped to establish.

○ They feel that their views are important.

○ It gives them a sense of ownership of the rules.

By having a sense of ownership of the rules and feeling that their views are important, the learners are more likely to adhere to them. Indeed, the role of managing the rules is often taken up by the learners themselves, with some being keen to point out to their peers when their behaviour is unacceptable.

Activity

When do you think the approach of negotiating ground rules cannot apply?

Comment

While negotiation of ground rules is always preferable, exceptions will arise when legislation or organisational policies are involved, for example when issues of equality and diversity and health and safety are involved.

SUMMARY OF KEY POINTS

This chapter has explored your understanding of ways in which you can create an inclusive teaching environment including:

○ how to motivate and support learners;

○ how to establish ground rules to provide a safe and positive learning environment;

○ the importance of supporting learners' development of their English, mathematics, ICT and wider skills.

Check your understanding

1   What is inclusive teaching and learning?

2   Write down at least three ways in which learners may differ.

3   Give an example of an appropriate teaching method for each of the cognitive, affective and psychomotor domains.

4   Why are ground rules important?

5   What is the most effective way of creating ground rules and why?

6   Why is it important to embed Functional Skills into lessons in the FE sector?

7   Outline three key points that you have learned from reading this chapter.

 TAKING IT FURTHER

Businessballs.com. Free VAK Learning Styles Test. [online] Available at: www.businessballs.com/vaklearningstylestest.htm

This website has a concise though useful learning styles questionnaire if you wish to explore your own learning preferences further.

Machin, L, Hindmarch, D, Murray, S and Richardson, T (2015) *A Complete Guide to the Level 4 Certificate in Education and Training.* 2nd ed. Northwich: Critical Publishing.

This is a key text if you wish to investigate any of the subjects covered in this book or intend to continue onto the CET. Chapter 6 gives a more in-depth look at all aspects of inclusive teaching and learning.

Sharrock, T (2015) *Embedding English and Maths: Practical Strategies for FE and Post-16 Tutors (Further Education).* Northwich: Critical Publishing.

Includes a range of practical strategies and ideas for embedding English and mathematics.

REFERENCES

Bloom, B S (ed) (1956) *Taxonomy of Educational Objectives: The Classification of Educational Goals. Handbook I: Cognitive Domain*. New York: David McKay.

Education & Training Foundation (ETF) (2014) *Professional Standards for Teachers and Trainers in Education and Training – England*. [onlinc] Available at: www.et-foundation.co.uk/supporting/support-practitioners/professional-standards/ (accessed December 2015).

The Equality ACT (2010). [online] Available at www.legislation.gov.uk/ukpga/2010/15/contents (accessed 24 February 2016).

Krathwohl, D R, Bloom, B S and Masia, B B (1964) *Taxonomy of Educational Objectives: The Classification of Educational Goals. Handbook II: The Affective Domain*. New York: David McKay.

Leitch, Lord S (2006) *The Leitch Review of Skills: Prosperity for All in the Global Economy – World Class Skills*. Final Report. London: The Stationery Office.

Machin, L, Hindmarch, D, Murray, S and Richardson, T (2015) *A Complete Guide to the Level 5 Diploma in Education and Training*. Northwich: Critical Publishing.

Simpson, E J (1966) The Classification of Educational Objectives: Psychomotor Domain. *Illinois Journal of Home Economics*, 10(4): 110–44.

3 Facilitating learning and development for individuals

Understanding principles and practices of one-to-one learning and development

Advantages and disadvantages of learning in a one-to-one situation

What is the purpose of individual learning?

The learning mentor

The role of the facilitator

Facilitating learning and development for individuals

Facilitating reflective one-to-one learning and development

The learning support assistant

Problem-based learning

Managing risks and safeguarding individuals

Professional responsibilities and safeguarding

INTRODUCTION

This chapter helps you to understand how to facilitate learning on a one-to-one basis. It also helps you to support individual learners in applying new knowledge and skills in practical contexts.

OBJECTIVES

This chapter covers the learning outcomes of the following AET optional units (Group B, level 3, 6 credits):

○ Facilitate learning and development for individuals (Learning and Development unit).

The chapter therefore develops your understanding of the following:

○ the principles and practices of one-to-one learning and development;

○ the ability to facilitate one-to-one learning and development;

○ the ability to assist individual learners in applying new knowledge and skills in practical contexts;

○ the ability to assist individual learners in reflecting on their learning and/or development.

See Table 1 at the front of the book for how this chapter covers aspects of the ETF (2014) standards.

STARTING POINT

What does facilitation mean to you?

Facilitation has been around since the 1960s, mainly through the work of Carl Rogers and Josephine Klein (Smith, 2009). A facilitator helps to make the learning happen, rather than teaching the subject, and in this sense is a strategy rather than a role. Many teachers use facilitation as part of their planned strategies for delivery. A facilitative approach supports the learners to gather the information and then reflect on what they have learned and how they can use it. Facilitation is seen as part of learning how to think and not being told what to think.

THE ROLE OF THE FACILITATOR

When working in FE you may often find yourself in a one-to-one situation with a learner. This may be because you are in a coaching role, a mentoring role, a support or tutoring role or maybe a specialist support role. You may be teaching work-based learning, where you are going into the workplace and working with learners on a one-to-one basis or you may devise classroom strategies that incorporate one-to-one facilitation with learners. Two of these roles, which can overlap, are discussed below.

The learning mentor

According to the National Careers Service (2015), a learning mentor helps learners with any difficulty they have with their learning. As a learning mentor, you could work in a school or a college, supporting learners of all abilities with issues like poor attendance; lack of self-confidence, self-esteem or motivation; failure to achieve their full potential; behavioural or emotional difficulties; difficulty settling into school or college; or personal difficulties. You would work with learners on a one-to-one basis outside of the classroom to:

○   *develop one-to-one mentoring relationships with students;*

○   *develop action plans for students and monitor their progress;*

○   *work closely with teachers and other professionals, like social workers, educational psychologists and education welfare officers.*

(National Careers Service, 2015)

The learning support assistant

Another role where you might work on a one-to-one basis with a learner is as a learning support assistant (LSA). As a teacher, you may have an LSA allocated to one or more of your learners.

An LSA is usually allocated to work with one learner in a group or on a one-to-one basis away from the group. The support is there to remove barriers to the learning that diminish the learner's ability to progress. An LSA role often means liaising closely with a teacher to support the learner in the best possible way. Wisker et al (2008) note that in an economic climate where there is less funding for education, one-to-one facilitation is used sparingly as it is costly.

> ### *Activity*
>
> Have you ever worked on a one-to-one basis with an individual and facilitated their learning?

Case study 1

Ben works for a private training organisation as a trainee training officer (assessor). He provides training in the hospitality sector and carries out teaching and learning assessments and reviews in the workplace with apprentices. Often there is only one apprentice in a workplace and this means Ben often works on a one-to-one basis with them.

Ben's training organisation does not just want the apprentices to learn about their own job, but also to learn about the industry or trade that they work in. To help with this, Ben often uses a facilitation approach. He expects the learner to find out about their own organisation as well as the wider industry to which they belong. Ben then supports the apprentice to understand how this fits in with the organisation that they work for. The training organisation wants to make sure that at the end of the course the apprentice's employer is happy with the work that the apprentice is doing. By using the facilitation approach, Ben feels he is helping to foster skills that the apprentice can then use in the workplace.

Activity

Why do you think workplaces do not want an apprentice to just learn about their own job?

WHAT IS THE PURPOSE OF INDIVIDUAL LEARNING?

In 1984, Benjamin Bloom carried out research with a group of university learners in the United States in order to explore differences in learning using three different methods of teaching:

○ conventional tutoring: learners are in groups of 30 per teacher with tests given periodically;

○ mastery learning: the same as conventional learning but with help to work on areas the learners have not got right in the tests and more formative assessment;

○ tutoring: one-to-one with a tutor with the same sort of summative and formative assessments as in mastery learning.

Bloom (1984) found that the tutored learners did best, with the mastery learners doing the next best and the conventionally tutored learners did the least well. The average tutored learner achieved better than 98 per cent of the conventionally tutored learners. It is up to teachers and facilitators to try to work out the best way to deliver teaching to a group that replicates the results of one-to-one sessions, without the significant costs involved.

Understanding the principles and practices of one-to-one learning and development

Many of the principles and practices of one-to-one learning are similar to group learning (see Chapter 4). Mutual respect and voluntary engagement are still essential. One principle that is easier to achieve in a one-to-one situation is that the learner's needs, culture and interests can be taken into consideration in the preparation of the lesson. In a group situation, setting ground rules with the learners is essential. It is equally essential to set ground rules in a one-to-one situation; otherwise, it may affect the learning. The learner needs to understand what is expected of them and you.

Some of the ground rules that you might discuss with a learner could include:

○ punctuality;

○ what work they need to complete outside of the classroom;

○ the need to listen to each other;

○ mutual respect;

○ the importance of being motivated;

○ switching off mobile phone(s) (when appropriate).

You could discuss the ground rules with the learner during one of your early meetings.

Advantages and disadvantages of learning in a one-to-one situation

Advantages

○ The learner has the attention of the facilitator.

○ You are able to give very personalised feedback and learning.

○ The learner can go at a pace that is appropriate for them.

○ They can make contributions or ask questions without worrying about what other learners will think.

○ The learner's strengths and areas for development can be focused upon.

○ There are fewer time constraints so they can go at their own pace and not feel pressured by the progress of other learners.

○ You can adapt the learning process to suit the learning style of the learner.

○ You can use appropriate topic-based learning.

○ Learning outcomes are tailored to the learner's needs.

○ Other learners' behaviour does not affect the learning taking place.

Disadvantages

○ Progress is often measured against other learners, so some stretch-and-challenge activities and learning may be missing.

○ The learning can be quite intense and tiring for the learner.

○ There are no other learners to bounce ideas off.

○ The learner might consciously or unconsciously turn the one-to-one sessions into counselling or 'moaning' sessions.

Activity

Have you had any one-to-one learning encounters with a teacher?

If so, what were the main advantages and disadvantages for you?

 Case study 2

Jenny is enrolled on the AET award. She decides she wants to do the following optional unit: Facilitate learning and development for individuals. As part of this unit she must be observed in a real work environment. She is currently working at a college in administration but has expressed an interest in working one-to-one to support a number of learners who have poor literacy skills. She has been given some learners (with a mentor to support her) and has just had her first one-to-one observation.

The observation generally went well. Jenny had planned quite a few activities and kept her learner on task the whole of the time. She had not planned on how she was going to assess the learning taking place. While the learner was completing a task given to him, Jenny sat and watched him. She also did not give the learner a time frame in which to complete his tasks. Jenny had him working for a complete hour. He did mention a few times in the session that he liked a particular football team.

After a discussion with the observer, Jenny reflected on a number of development points for future lessons. Instead of watching the learner complete a task, she is going to prepare for the next task – to take the stress off him. She decided she needed to specify a time frame to help the learner know how deep she wanted him to go with a written task. This would also stop him from rushing through the task because he thought she was waiting to do the next exercise. She also reflected that perhaps a quick few minutes off task half way through the session would refresh the learner and help him to take in the information. Jenny has decided to incorporate the football team as a topic into future lessons, where appropriate, to stimulate the learner's interest.

Activity

In Case Study 2, what else could Jenny have done to make sure the learning outcomes were met?

There is a requirement to undertake observed and assessed practice in a real work environment for the following optional units from the Learning and Development suite that are included in this qualification:

Facilitate learning and development for individuals (level 3);

Facilitate learning and development in groups (level 3).

For these units, practice should be in the appropriate context with groups of learners or with individual learners. The number of hours of practice required and the number of hours to be observed and assessed are not specified.

LSIS (2013)

FACILITATING REFLECTIVE ONE-TO-ONE LEARNING AND DEVELOPMENT

If you only have one learner this does not mean that you do not need to vary your delivery strategy. There are facilitation methods you can use to help meet the learning and development needs of an individual learner.

Firstly, at the start of a topic or each lesson you and the learner need to agree on the learning outcomes and adjust them, if needed, to suit the intended outcome of the one-to-one session. It is much easier to teach a learner who understands what is required of them and buys into the lesson. By setting clear goals the learners and the facilitator are easily able to see if the learning outcomes have been met. When planning a one-to-one lesson, differentiation can still be used; when preparing activities you may be unsure if the learner will be able to cope with what has been set. In this case, you might create a scaffolded version of the activity or provide some prompt words to be used if needed. This could be done either before the session or during the session.

Do not rule out discussions and paired activities; remember that there is another person in the room – you – so activities that need more than one learner can still go ahead, with you taking part. You do need to structure the discussion, otherwise it could go off track or important information could be missed out. Make sure that you do not influence the learner with regard to your own assumptions as you do not want to create a mini-me version of yourself. Social media, joining in or following a debate online (this would need to be monitored for content) are also useful strategies for one-to-one learning encounters. If you have two or more individual learners working on a similar task you could also record or note down their thoughts and share them with another learner (with their permission).

Ice-breakers can be particularly useful during the first session as they can help to erase any initial tension that the learner may have about the one-to-one meetings. An energiser can be used to freshen up the learner if you notice that they are starting to tire. This is an activity that involves movement (see Taking it Further). Be flexible; if an activity is not working then you can change it very swiftly and easily. Similarly, if a learner is struggling with something, you can swap to another activity and then come back to the other task at a later time. Give the learner time to think and always have a plenary session at the end of the lesson to consolidate learning.

Be an active listener; Wisker et al (2013) suggest that the facilitator has to be totally aligned with the learner, not just hearing what they say on the surface but also picking up on any undertones and making sure your body language and verbal responses show that you are listening. However, remember that different cultures use different body language and make sure you are not causing offence (Wisker et al, 2013). Make sure you praise the learner but try not to overpraise.

○ *Praise learners' efforts and specific work strategies ("process praise") and outcomes when they do well, rather than praising them for their intelligence ("person praise").*

○ *Discourage learners from attributing successes and failures to things over which they have no control (poor luck, or how smart or "dumb" they are).*

○ *Don't offer praise for trivial accomplishments or weak efforts.*

○ *Don't inflate praise, particularly for learners with low self-esteem.*

APA (2013, p 1)

It is important that you support your learner(s) in developing their ability to critically reflect. As with a group you can do this by giving the learner a number of questions before giving them a task to complete. This can then be followed up with deeper level questions, as appropriate to the learner's needs. You can also provide another side to a debate or find another viewpoint online. Be aware that there might be issues to do with the learner that you know little or nothing about and that some topics might be sensitive to the learner. Also, give them plenty of time to answer questions and to reflect on the learning; teachers can have a habit of answering their own questions rather too quickly. Importantly, ensure that any resources you use are suitable for the learner as resources used for larger groups may need to be adapted to suit the individual learner's needs.

A useful strategy is to ask them to bring along some resources to use in the lesson. They could, for example, bring a favourite sport magazine that you could then use or perhaps you could ask them to take five photos on the way to the lesson where words are being used in an interesting or different way (obviously you would check beforehand to see if the learner had a camera on their phone). Using these resources as part of the one-to-one session can enhance the learner's motivation as well as their ability to learn.

> ### Activity
>
> Why would bringing in their own resources enhance the learner's motivation and learning?

Some of the facilitation methods you would normally associate with groups can still be adapted to a one-to-one situation. For example:

○ meta-planning, where you ask the learner to put their ideas down on Post-it notes, then arrange them on a wall into subgroups to see if the ideas naturally fall into different categories, can be a good learning strategy to use;

○ pre- and post-exercise quizzes; give the learner a quiz about what they know about a topic before starting an activity and then again at the end to see the change in knowledge.

PROBLEM-BASED LEARNING

Problem-based learning, often referred to as PBL, is very learner-centred and was developed initially in the 1960s for medical training (Woods, 2015). PBL can fit well with facilitation. Giving a learner a real problem to solve will help them to develop the skills, knowledge and understanding necessary to work through the problem. Usually PBL is run with groups but there is no reason why it cannot work well on a one-to-one basis – especially when using technology enhanced learning (TEL). The learner will identify what they already know about how to solve the problem, what they need to know and how they are going to access the information. You can also scaffold the problem by breaking it down into stages, providing support to help the learner find the 'right' answer.

There are some very good examples on the internet of PBL problems in all subjects at all levels. NASA has some excellent environment-based problems that are transferable to many subjects – see Taking it further at the end of this chapter.

Table 3.1 The theory of problem-based learning

Cognitive constructivism (Piaget)	Social constructivism (Vygotsky)
Definition: The learner adds new information to existing knowledge, enabling them to make the appropriate cognitive changes to accommodate that information. Piaget (1972)	*Definition: emphasises the collaborative nature of much learning.* Vygotsky (1978)

Table 3.1 (cont.)

Cognitive constructivism (Piaget)	Social constructivism (Vygotsky)
Uses primary data	Authentic problems; learning environments reflect real-world complexities
Learner autonomy; thinking and learning responsibility in learners' hands to foster ownership	Team choice and common interests; builds on common interests and experiences within a learning group, and gives some choice to that group; learning activities are 'relevant, meaningful'
Meaningfulness and personal motivation; learning related to personal ideas and experiences	Encourages learner elaboration/justification for their responses through discussion, questioning, group presentations
Information organised around concepts, problems, questions and themes	Encourages reflection
Builds on prior knowledge and addresses misconceptions	Teacher explanations and support provide hints, prompts, cues and clarifications where requested to solve the problem
Questioning; promotes individual inquiry with open-ended questions; encourages question-asking behaviour	Multiple viewpoints; fosters multiple ways of understanding a problem

Stanford University (2014a, p 5)

PBL can also be regarded as a mix of social constructivist and cognitive theories as proposed by Piaget (1972) and Vygotsky (1978). Table 3.1 demonstrates this mix; it refers to group as well as one-to-one PBL.

MANAGING RISKS AND SAFEGUARDING INDIVIDUALS

For a one-to-one session, there are still decisions to be made about the layout of the room, such as where the learner is going to sit and where you are going to sit. This can be vital to the delivery of the lesson and if you let the learner dictate where they sit, you might end up too close to them or with some sort of barrier between you which is not conducive to learning.

Professional responsibilities and safeguarding

The ETF standards (2014) include two areas that you must always keep in mind when working one-to-one:

11. *Manage and promote positive learner behaviour.*

12. *Understand the teaching and professional role and your responsibilities.*

You need to ensure the safety of the learner and your own safety. If you are working in an educational establishment, you will have covered safeguarding training so make yourself aware of any issues that the educational establishment knows about the learner that are pertinent to the learning situation – for example, a recent bereavement of a close relative, family illness or financial worries. In these circumstances, it might not be appropriate to then bring the family tree in as a topic. The one-to-one situation can be quite an intimate situation and you need to take this into consideration when planning one-to-one sessions. Consider:

○   where are you meeting?

○   will there be other people about?

○   does the learner have easy access to necessary facilities (food, water, toilets)?

○   if you are meeting in the evening, will there be other people around when you have finished the session?

○   do security staff know where you are so they can leave lights on in corridors and car parks?

It is important that you also keep the classroom door open and make other teachers or staff aware that you are meeting one-to-one with a learner and why, especially if this is not part of the normal timetable.

You should check if your organisation has a lone working policy and if so make sure you know what it entails. Make sure you report any inappropriate learner behaviour to a line manager as soon as possible. Remember that you need to be as professional when you are with one student as you are when you are with a group of students. Reflect on your professional role when you are in the classroom: are you performing the function that has been set for you with the learner? If your function is primarily to facilitate learning but you find yourself listening to the learner's problems for most of the lesson or get involved in sorting them out, then you need to reflect on your professional role; your role is that of a teacher and beyond the boundaries of this you need to seek other support for the learner. Find out what support is available in the organisation and then talk to the learner about how they can access that support.

Activity

What else might you do to ensure that both the learner and teacher are safe during a one-to-one learning encounter?

SUMMARY OF KEY POINTS

○   When facilitating learning and development for individuals, the flexibility of the learning activities is very important.

○   You must not dismiss strategies as only working in a group situation; think how they can be adapted to work in the one-to-one situation.

○   Each learner will need different strategies and support.

○   Facilitation is not the only way of delivering learning to individuals.

Check your understanding

1   What do you think are the three most important advantages of one-to-one learning?

2   What do you think could be the three worst disadvantages of one-to-one learning?

3   What is problem-based learning?

4   Do you understand your professional boundaries when working one-to-one with a learner?

5   Outline three key points that you have learned from reading this chapter.

 TAKING IT FURTHER

For a teacher's anecdotal perspective on using PBL in the classroom in the USA: www.theguardian.com/teacher-network/teacher-blog/2013/dec/08/project-based-learning-high-tech-high-teacher

This is an excellent site for PBL resources from NASA for use in the classroom. Although it is only based around the environment, it could be used in a number of different situations: http://ete.cet.edu/modules/modules.html

A very thorough teacher's guide to project-based learning but which does need adapting more for one-to-one facilitation is: http://www.innovationunit.org/sites/default/files/Teacher's%20Guide%20to%20Project-based%20Learning.pdf

REFERENCES

Bloom, B (1984) The 2 Sigma Problem: The Search for Methods of Group Instruction as Effective as One-to-one Tutoring. *Educational Researcher,* 13(6): 4–16.

Dwyer, C et al (2015) *Using Praise to Enhance Learner Resilience and Learning Outcomes.* Washington: American Psychological Association.

Education & Training Foundation (ETF) (2014) *Professional Standards for Teachers and Trainers in Education and Training – England.* [online] Available at: www.et-foundation.co.uk/supporting/support-practitioners/professional-standards/ (accessed December 2015).

Learning Skills Improvement Services (LSIS) (2013) *Teaching and Training Qualifications for the Further Education and Skills Sector in England: Guidance for Employees and Practitioners*. Coventry: LSIS.

National Careers Service (2015) *Learning Mentor*. [online] Available at: https://nationalcareersservice.direct.gov.uk/advice/planning/jobprofiles/Pages/learningmentor.aspx (accessed December 2015).

Piaget, J (1972) *Psychology of the Child.* New York: Basic Books.

Smith, M (2009) Facilitating Learning and Change in Groups and Group Sessions. *The Encyclopaedia of Informal Education.* [online] Available at: www.infed.org/mobi/facilitating-learning-and-change-in-groups-and-group-sessions/ (accessed December 2015).

Stanford University (2014) *Problem-based Learning Theory.* [online] Available at: http://ldt.stanford.edu/~jeepark/jeepark+portfolio/PBL/theory.htm (accessed December 2015).

Wisker, G et al (2008) *Working One-to-One with Learners: Supervising, Coaching, Mentoring, and Personal Tutoring.* Abingdon: Routledge.

Woods, D (2015) *Problem-based Learning.* [online] Available at: http://chemeng.mcmaster.ca/problem-based-learning (accessed December 2015).

Vygotsky, L (1978) *Mind in Society: Development of Higher Psychological Processes* Harvard: Harvard University Press.

4 Facilitating learning and development in groups

Disadvantages of learning within groups

Advantages of learning within groups

Supporting learners to apply new knowledge and skills in practical contexts

The role of the teacher as a facilitator

Understanding the principles and practices of learning and development in groups

Determining the size of learning groups

Facilitating learning and development in groups

The purpose of group learning and development

Facilitating group work

Delivery of learning and development to reflect group dynamics

Assisting learners to reflect on their learning and development in groups

Arranging the learning environment to accommodate groups

Recognising and reinforcing supportive behaviours and responses

Managing risks and safeguarding individuals in groups

INTRODUCTION

This chapter develops your understanding of facilitating learning and development in groups. This will enable you to implement effective strategies that will help your learners to explore subject matter and learn from and with their peers.

OBJECTIVES

This chapter covers the learning outcomes of the following AET optional units (Group B, level 3, 6 credits):

o   Facilitate learning and development in groups (Learning and Development unit).

The chapter therefore develops your understanding of the following:

o   the principles and practices of learning and development in groups;

o   the ability to facilitate learning and development in groups;

o   the ability to assist groups to apply new knowledge and skills in practical contexts;

o   the ability to assist learners to reflect on their learning and development undertaken in groups.

See Table 1 at the front of the book for how this chapter covers aspects of the ETF (2014) standards.

STARTING POINT

What do you think facilitation means?

Facilitation, as a strategy for learning, is not new to teachers. During the 1960s, Klein's work in particular raised the potential benefit of using a facilitative approach within schools in the UK. Currently, with the growth in research about teaching and learning as well as the greater emphasis of regulatory bodies (Ofsted, for example) on learning rather than teaching, facilitation is a popular choice as a strategy used by teachers.

THE ROLE OF THE TEACHER AS A FACILITATOR

As a teacher you will have many roles and one of these is that of a facilitator. This means that rather than teaching, ie standing at the front of the classroom and giving learners topic information, you will manage and support a learning group during their engagement in the activities you have set for them. In doing this you are maximising the group's effectiveness and capacity for learning (Schwarz, 2002).

Activity

Can you provide two examples of when you have facilitated a group activity?

UNDERSTANDING THE PRINCIPLES AND PRACTICES OF LEARNING AND DEVELOPMENT IN GROUPS

A principle (or a set of principles) is a belief, idea, rule or chain of reasoning that serves as a foundation and guide for individuals and subsequently groups and organisations.

Prominent writers about group learning (for example, Brookfield, 2005; Lave and Wenger, 2003) suggest that when learning in groups attention should be given to principles (or ground rules) for the group. Some suggestions of principles are provided in

Table 4.1 Examples of principles that can support efficient and effective group learning

Principle	Explanation
Mutual respect	This would include making sure that everyone's opinion was valued and that each group member had an opportunity to speak and to be heard.
Voluntary engagement	This would mean that no individual was forced to participate.
Agreed objectives	Being part of a team where all are learning towards the same outcome can be very motivational and socially as well as educationally rewarding.

Table 4.1 below.

It is up to you as a teacher to decide when the best time would be to discuss the principles to be upheld by the group.

Activity

What might happen to a learning group if no principles are in place?

Comment

If some learners in a group believe that their opinions are not being taken seriously, or that no one is listening to them, they will become demotivated and disengaged. Some learners may start to misbehave and cause others to do likewise if there is no facilitator to manage them and no ground rules have been set.

THE PURPOSE OF GROUP LEARNING AND DEVELOPMENT

As with any task, when you plan an activity for your learners that involves group work you need to consider:

○   the learning purpose of the activity;

○   if the activity is the most appropriate for the learning purpose – taking account of the conditions and constraints of the learning environment;

○   if the purpose of the learning activity is solely related to the subject topic or if it will support the development of social relationships and a community of practice.

It is important that all learners know what the learning purpose of the task is and what the objectives of the task are, ie what they need to have achieved by the end of the group task. The best approach is to tell your learners verbally and also in writing (as part of your presentation or in a work task given to the learners) what the objectives are. Without guidance learners can quickly become confused and/or disengaged.

SUPPORTING LEARNERS TO APPLY NEW KNOWLEDGE AND SKILLS IN PRACTICAL CONTEXTS

One of the key tasks of facilitators and facilitating is to help learners to remain committed to the task they are doing and to support them in that process (Egan, 2006). This can be done using a variety of facilitation styles. For example, adopting a directive style at the beginning of a group learning task can be beneficial as it helps the group to understand and to focus on the task given to them. Once the group have begun to learn and work together you may want to change your facilitation approach to a more consultative one. When you visit some groups you may want to use a Socratic questioning style whereas with others a better approach might be to leave them to it; as a teacher and a facilitator you will need to make a judgement on what the best approach is for your learners' needs. Whatever style you use it should be one that encourages all learners to contribute to the task given.

Activity

Why do you think it is important to explain what is expected of each learner in a group?

Comment

It is important that all learners get an opportunity to speak and/or to contribute to the session in some way. Alongside establishing the group task you will need to give instructions for any individual tasks; for example, you may want some of the learners in the group to take notes or to be the timekeeper.

Advantages of learning within groups

Engaging in group activities is one way in which individual learners can develop new knowledge or consolidate the current knowledge that they have about the topic being discussed. Learning in groups can also challenge learners' pre-held opinions about the topic or individuals within the group.

Other advantages of learning in a group include:

o   increased motivation due to carrying out learning activities with others;

o   tasks can be accomplished more speedily and effectively as more learners are involved;

o   development of learners' social and communication skills;

o   development of learners' listening and speaking skills;

o   learners' development of positive behaviours through modelling those of others in the group;

o   ability to draw on more information and experiences than one individual learner would possess, which can result in new or better ideas and solutions; develops problem-solving skills;

o   learners will bring different skills to the group and this can improve the thoroughness of how a task is undertaken and completed;

o   shared learning can enhance deep rather than surface learning;

o   sustained and/or increased energy;

o   feelings of belonging (noted as important to learning by Abraham Maslow, 1943).

Activity

o   Can you come up with any other advantages to those given above regarding learning within a group? Make a list.

o   Provide an example of when you have developed a learning concept and/or developed a new skill through being engaged in a group activity.

Disadvantages of learning within groups

As you might expect, alongside the many advantages that learners have when learning in groups there are some, if perhaps fewer, disadvantages. For example, learning in groups can result in groupthink. Groupthink is when individuals think as a group and this thinking can be influenced by the most dynamic members of the group. Groupthink can reduce the degree of critical thinking that occurs, and limitations and defects in learners' thinking can take place.

Other disadvantages of learning in a group include:

○ some learners may feel that they are not given an opportunity to speak – they wait for a space to speak but the more dynamic members of the group fill that space;

○ the larger the group, the less time per person is available and the fewer opportunities each member will likely have to contribute to discussions;

○ some learners may not wish to share their views if they consider them to be dissimilar to those shared by other, perhaps more confident or well-liked, members of the group;

○ group work can be time consuming and may restrict the number of other teaching and learning activities that can be delivered in a session;

○ learners may develop negative behaviours modelled by others in the group;

○ conflict and misunderstandings can occur between individual members in the group;

○ some learners may exert less effort than others; this is called social loafing and can create tensions in a group due to the unequal distribution of the workload;

○ learners' different styles of learning could create conflict.

Activity

○ Can you think of any other disadvantages of learning in a group? Make a list.

○ Have you ever been in a group that had social loafers; if so, how did their behaviour affect the other individuals in the group?

 Case study

Djen, a trainee teacher, was being observed for the first time. He had planned a detailed lesson that he thought would be suitable for a group of 20 business studies students, aged 16–18. The topic was relating to the marketing mix. Having set out the objectives for the lesson, Djen split the group into five groups of four students and asked each of them to come up with ideas for marketing a new product. The result was chaos.

The observer told Djen that the group activity had gone badly due to a lack of direction beyond the broad question about marketing a new product. The observer suggested that Djen could have given each group two or three questions to focus on (either the same or different for each group). Another suggestion was that a group leader and perhaps a scribe could have been appointed. Finally, the observer also suggested that Djen, in his role as a facilitator for the group activity, could have given the group a time countdown so that they knew that it was time to provide the outcome of their discussion.

Activity

In the case study above what could Djen have done to make sure that the group activity was more successful?

FACILITATING GROUP WORK

As a teacher you need to ensure that each learner is making progress according to their individual ability (see Chapter 2 about differentiation) and therefore it is crucial that you have strategies that can support the progress of the individual as well as the efficiency of the group and the task given. When deciding how to break up your whole class group into smaller subgroups you will need to consider:

○   the learning purpose of the activity;

○   the best size for each of the groups for the learning purpose;

○   the influence that individuals might have on the group dynamics;

○   how the learning environment can be arranged to accommodate the groups and the type of task set;

○   how the activity will maintain and/or enhance individuals' attention and motivation.

Determining the size of learning groups

Both small and large groups have advantages and disadvantages.

Large learning groups

A large learning group may refer to the whole class that you are teaching or it may be that you have split the whole class group into several smaller, but still large, learning groups.

> ### *Activity*
>
> ○ What do you think the minimum number of students should be in a large learning group?
>
> ○ What do you think the maximum number of students should be in a large learning group?

Although there is no exact number which defines whether a group is a large one, the general opinion is that five to seven students is about right (Jacques and Salmon, 2007, p 25).

A feature of large groups is the diversity of knowledge and experience that each individual brings to the group which, in turn, supports the development and growth of other individuals. Conversely, this diversity can restrict decision making for a larger group due to the variety of views held or, as can happen, lead to splinter groups developing within the larger group.

Small learning groups

Three or four students in a group is about the right number for a small group. Groups of this size are useful for enabling all learners to make an equal contribution to the discussion; this can build their confidence and experience of speaking. Also, as all learners are at the centre of the discussion they all take ownership of the outcome of the discussion. However, the group is unlikely to be as diverse as a larger group, thereby reducing opportunities for individual assumptions to be challenged by those holding different views.

Delivery of learning and development to reflect group dynamics

Facilitating group activities and learning does not negate your responsibilities as a teacher, and you are required to manage the learning and the behaviour of the group. Some groups will be more congenial and collaborative than others. How individuals relate to others in the group influences the group dynamics which can ultimately influence the amount and depth of learning that occurs as well as what is learned. A popular model regarding the various stages of group development is Bruce Tuckman's model, detailed below.

○ Forming: Individuals come together and gradually get to know each other.

○ Storming: Individuals vie for their position and their role in the group.

○ Norming: Individuals come together and work as a collective, positions are accepted and group norms are established.

○ Performing: Individuals carry out tasks in order to reach goals and targets.

○ Adjourning: The team, for a variety of reasons, disband.

(Smith, 2005)

It is likely that learners will be with different learners each time you set a group task. However, all of them belong to the larger class group and they will develop a group culture with group dynamics in this whole group which will then be taken with them into the learning groups. However, the dynamics might be different or become different over a period of time from when the whole class is together.

> ## Activity
>
> Do you think Tuckman's model is a fairly accurate description of any group(s) to which you have belonged?

Arranging the learning environment to accommodate groups

An administrator or a manager will have allocated you a room for each of your classes. While occasionally it may be possible to swap with another teacher so that you can carry out a particular activity, it will be the room that you are allocated that you will need to consider when planning your sessions. You need to think about the following:

○ the time you have before the session to change, if necessary, the layout of the room;

○ the time you have following a session to change the layout back to how it was before your session;

○ if any changes to the layout impact on any other activities and/or tasks that you will be giving your learners during the session. For example, will they all be facing forward towards you when you are talking to them? If some will have their backs to you what can you do about this?

You will need to keep all learners in a group focused on the task given to them. You can do this by asking questions and providing some initial feedback when, as required, you visit each of the groups. You can also do this by ensuring that their contributions are valued and are disseminated in a follow-up activity to the other groups.

MANAGING RISKS AND SAFEGUARDING INDIVIDUALS IN GROUPS

The safeguarding of your learners is an important consideration when you are planning learning activities. If you are planning a group activity you will need to consider if there are any issues that you need to know about, for example any bullying or misbehaviour by learners in the same group. If you are planning a group activity with a group that you have never taught before it is advisable, if possible, to ask another teacher or member of staff if there are any issues with the learners that you ought to know about. Safeguarding learners also includes managing the behaviour of the learners in the groups.

RECOGNISING AND REINFORCING SUPPORTIVE BEHAVIOURS AND RESPONSES

As a teacher, having incorporated group learning activities into your class sessions, you will need to facilitate these activities and to manage the behaviour of the individuals in each of the groups (see Chapters 1 and 2 for further information about this). One useful strategy, as noted earlier in this chapter, is to implement some ground rules which, for example, could include all members of the group being:

○   respectful towards each other;

○   supportive of each other;

○   prepared to listen to others, even when they may not agree with what is said by another person;

○   non-judgemental.

Another strategy (as noted earlier in the chapter) is to allocate different members of the group a task to do; as well as being motivational this can also be linked to positive behaviour between all members of the group.

ASSISTING LEARNERS TO REFLECT ON THEIR LEARNING AND DEVELOPMENT IN GROUPS

According to Brookfield (2005), facilitation aims to foster critical reflection through adopting teaching and learning strategies that require learners to find a solution and/or answers to the tasks presented or the questions asked.

> ### *Activity*
>
> How can you encourage critical reflection in group learning?

Once you have decided on the purpose of the group learning task you need to decide the best approach to use to encourage deep, rather than surface, learning. For example, you can do this by giving learners a list of set questions to consider during the completion of the task and/or by prompting further discussion when you visit each of the groups as part of your role as a facilitator. As a facilitator you have the privileged position of being able to assist in developing the mental models of the learners, ie challenging learners' assumptions. This can be done by:

○   asking probing questions;

○   asking the other groups their opinion;

○   providing an alternative viewpoint;

○   drawing on different examples that challenge the learners' assumptions.

As with other learning activities that you set your learners you need to provide feedback to each group either during the activity or afterwards (or both). Feedback adds further value to the learning activity and if it incorporates a question and answer session also provides an opportunity to assess individual learning.

Above all, you need to check if the activity has been successful for the learning purpose.

○ Have the learners learned what you intended them to through the activity planned?

○ Are the learners aware of the knowledge or skill that they have developed (a reward and/or consequence of engaging in the activity should be new or consolidated learning)?

SUMMARY OF KEY POINTS

The approaches you use to facilitate group learning will be influenced by:

○ the learning purpose of the group activity;

○ the room and resources that are available to you;

○ consideration of the diverse natures of the learners and how these may influence the learning encounters;

○ your ability to manage the size of the groups (for example, value individuals, ask questions, provide feedback).

 Check your understanding

1 Explain what is meant by the term *facilitator*.

2 What are three advantages to learners working in groups?

3 What are three disadvantages to learners working in groups?

4 Give an example of an activity that could be approached through a group activity.

5 Why is it important to set ground rules when learners are working in groups?

6 Outline three key points that you have learned from reading this chapter.

TAKING IT FURTHER

Machin, L, Hindmarch, D, Murray, S and Richardson, T (2015) *A Complete Guide to the Level 4 Certificate in Education*. 2nd ed. Northwich: Critical Publishing.

This book provides you with further information about the key topics covered at level 3 and, through its coverage of the learning outcomes for the CET qualification, can support your development at level 4.

Scruton, J and Ferguson, B (2014) *Teaching and Supporting Adult Learners*. Northwich: Critical Publishing.

This book is written for teachers who want to develop their skills and knowledge in supporting adult learners. It is designed to help you create an inclusive approach to teaching and enhance the experiences of you and your learners.

Spenceley, L (2014) *Inclusion in Further Education*. Northwich: Critical Publishing.

This book provides a critical understanding of the concept of inclusion in a variety of settings and encourages you to consider and challenge assumptions.

REFERENCES

Brookfield, S (2005) *The Power of Critical Theory for Adult Learning and Teaching*. Berkshire: Open University Press.

Education & Training Foundation (ETF) (2014) *Professional Standards for Teachers and Trainers in Education and Training – England*. [online] Available at: www.et-foundation. co.uk/supporting/support-practitioners/professional-standards/ (accessed January 2016).

Egan, G (2006) *The Skilled Helper: A Problem-Management and Opportunity-Development Approach to Helping*. Belmont, CA: Thomson/Brooks Cole.

Jacques, D and Salmon, G (2007). *Learning in Groups: A Handbook for Face-to-Face and Online Environments*. 4th ed. Abingdon: Routledge.

Maslow, A (1943) A Theory of Human Motivation. *Psychological Review*, 50(4), pp 370–96.

Schwarz, R M (2002) *The Skilled Facilitator: A Comprehensive Resource for Consultants, Facilitators, Managers, Trainers and Coaches*. 2nd ed. San Francisco: Jossey-Bass.

Smith, M K (2005) *Bruce W. Tuckman – Forming, Storming, Norming and Performing in Groups*. [online] Available at: http://infed.org/mobi/bruce-w-tuckman-forming-storming-norming-and-performing-in-groups/ (accessed October 2015).

Smith, M K (2009) *Facilitating Learning and Change in Groups and Group Sessions*. [online] Available at: www.infed.org/mobi/facilitating-learning-and-change-in-groups-and-group-sessions/ (accessed November 2015).

5 Principles and practices of assessment

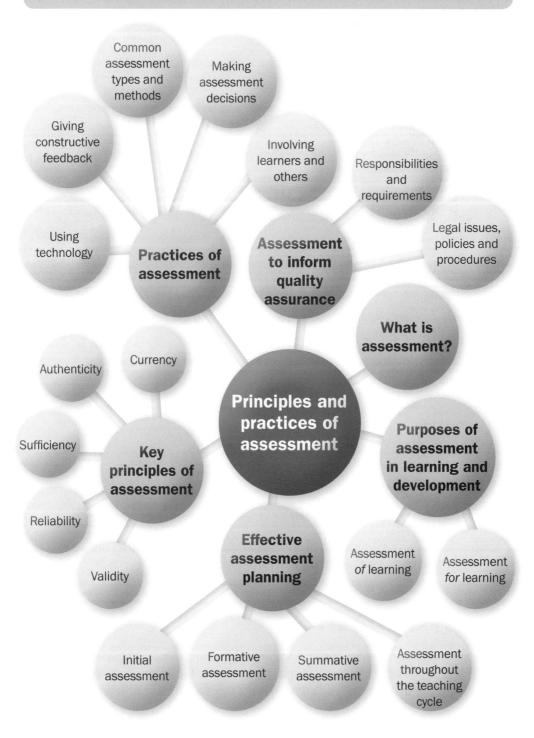

Common assessment types and methods

Making assessment decisions

Giving constructive feedback

Involving learners and others

Responsibilities and requirements

Using technology

Practices of assessment

Assessment to inform quality assurance

Legal issues, policies and procedures

Authenticity

Currency

What is assessment?

Sufficiency

Key principles of assessment

Principles and practices of assessment

Purposes of assessment in learning and development

Reliability

Validity

Effective assessment planning

Assessment of learning

Assessment for learning

Initial assessment

Formative assessment

Summative assessment

Assessment throughout the teaching cycle

INTRODUCTION

This chapter develops your understanding of assessment principles. This will help you to implement effective assessment into your everyday practice.

OBJECTIVES

This chapter covers the learning outcomes of the following AET optional units (Group C, level 3, 3 credits each):

- Understanding assessment in education and training (Education and Training unit).

- Understanding the principles and practices of assessment (Learning and Development unit).

The chapter therefore develops your understanding of the following:

- key principles and requirements of assessment;

- common types and methods of assessment;

- effective assessment planning;

- involving learners and others in the assessment process;

- giving constructive feedback and making assessment decisions;

- assessment record-keeping requirements in education and training;

- assessment to inform quality assurance.

See *Table 1 at the front of the book for how this chapter covers aspects of the ETF (2014) standards.*

STARTING POINT

What do you already know about assessment?

- Can you list at least four different strategies that are used for assessment purposes?

WHAT IS ASSESSMENT?

Assessment can be considered to be the practice of making a judgement about the knowledge and skills of a learner in relation to their study focus. It can assess the extent of a learner's current capabilities, further development needs and future potential.

Activity

As a learner you will have been assessed many times. Spend a few moments listing the key assessments during your life so far.

Comment

Your answer may have included formal assessments such as GCSEs and A levels or a driving test, and informal assessments such as in-class teacher-led question and answer activities during your school or college days.

PURPOSES OF ASSESSMENT IN LEARNING AND DEVELOPMENT

Activity

Why do you need to assess learners?

Consider the potential benefits for your learners, your own professional practice and your organisation.

The benefits of assessment include the following:

Benefits to learners:

○ awareness of their progress, strengths and future development needs;

○ reflection on their approaches to learning, leading to taking greater personal responsibility. With your constructive support, poor results could prompt reflection on what they need to change, for example better attendance, attitudes towards study, class contributions, homework completion and so on;

○ achieving academic credits, certificates or qualifications. This can enable further academic progression as well as promote employment and career opportunities;

○ increased personal self-esteem motivating further study resulting from assessment success. This can be especially relevant for learners who may not have achieved academic success at school.

Benefits to teachers:

○ ensuring learners are on the correct course through a process of initial assessment carried out prior to the start of a course. By checking the current skills of a learner from the very beginning you are ensuring that they are capable of success;

○ identifying any special educational needs and disabilities. Awareness of learners' specific difficulties can help them gain the required support. It can also inform changes to your teaching technique and resources to better meet learners' identified needs;

○ checking learning of individuals and groups; this will inform changes to your future teaching content and teaching strategies.

Benefits to the organisation:

○ improving results promotes recruitment, giving your organisation's marketing team clear evidence of success to attract new learners;

○ data for quality assurance – comparing results with other teachers, departments and organisation to ascertain the relative quality of your provision;

○ evidence of learner progress and achievement for external quality bodies such as Ofsted and, if you are delivering higher education courses at your organisation, the Quality Assurance Agency (QAA).

There are two key approaches to assessment: assessment *of* learning and assessment *for* learning.

Assessment *of* learning

Assessment of learning (AoL) covers what is traditionally associated with a final assessment, for example:

○ formal examinations or tests, usually at the end of a module or course;

○ teacher- or examiner-led marking;

○ clear judgement in terms of pass/fail or a grade.

AoL focuses on judgement: whether the learner has reached the required grade, standard or learning outcomes in order to pass a test. It therefore tends to be **summative** assessment – that is, assessment which is completed at the end of a period of learning, providing learners, teachers and other stakeholders (parents, the organisation and so on) with a clear judgement in terms of success or failure to achieve a required standard. AoL is the process used to judge whether a learner has passed a module or achieved a qualification. Qualifications are beneficial to learners as they provide clear and verifiable evidence of achievement which may enable further academic or career development.

However, you have to be careful that your enthusiasm for learners' success and improving or maintaining achievement statistics does not lead to assessment-led learning. This is where a teacher puts too much focus on assessment practice at the expense of developing the learners' subject expertise, motivation and broader employability skills. While learners need to practise tests to understand the requirements, too much of this can be boring and demotivating – to the extent where learners lose interest, misbehave and potentially achieve worse results.

In summary, successful teachers find a balance between sufficient assessment practice, so that their learners are aware of the course's requirements, and the learning activities used to develop their overall subject knowledge and motivation. Regular opportunities to discuss and listen to your learners can help you find this balance; many learners welcome the chance to voice their concerns and ideas for improvement.

Assessment *for* learning

Assessment for learning (AfL) emphasises the importance of **formative** assessment throughout the learning process. Formative assessment relates to your everyday assessment of learners during your classes. For example, asking your learners questions during class time or getting them to reflect on the quality of their work at the end of a workshop is formative assessment; you are checking their understanding of key ideas prior to any important summative exams and tests. Black and Wiliam (1998) have written extensively about the benefits associated with AfL when applied systematically throughout the whole organisation. AfL is therefore a concept of using assessment for more than judgement purposes, but as an integral part of learners' individual academic, social and employability development.

For learners, AfL promotes:

o regular and frequent formative assessment processes to raise awareness of current ability and progress;

o active learner participation in assessment and feedback;

o reflection on personal abilities and prioritised development needs;

o personal responsibility for their development;

o social learning through giving feedback to support the progress of learners and peers.

AfL emphasises the value of such formative assessment processes in terms of promoting achievement as well as learners' personal responsibility for their own development and success.

> ### *Activity*
>
> o List at least three strategies that could be used when you are making an assessment of learning.
>
> o List at least three strategies that could be used when you are assessing for learning.

EFFECTIVE ASSESSMENT PLANNING

For assessment to be effective, it needs to be considered as a key part of your planning process so that it is integral to your practice and the learners' experiences throughout the course.

Initial assessment

Your learners possess a range of differing experiences, qualifications, knowledge and skills which might be relevant to your course. They may also have specific needs or requirements which need to be identified prior to the beginning of the course in order to give them the best chance of success.

Initial assessment (IA) should therefore take place prior to enrolment to ensure learners do not start a course which they do not have the ability to complete. This also informs you about the individual and group skill levels prior to the beginning of the course, enabling you to make changes to your teaching plans to best meet their needs.

IA should therefore:

○ provide evidence of a learner's suitability for the course;

○ inform learners of their current ability, development needs;

○ inform planning in terms of group and individual abilities.

If a learner does not possess the required qualifications, skills or aptitude, they need to be directed to a more appropriate course or alternative provision.

If a learner has a special educational need (SEN) your organisation has to adhere to the SEND (Special Educational Needs and Disabilities) Code of Practice (DfE, 2015). This means that specific requirements must be identified in order to plan and negotiate reasonable adjustments to provide appropriate support (see the reasonable adjustments section).

Formative assessment

Formative assessment takes place throughout your lessons when you are checking understanding. Ensure that when you plan your lessons you consider how you are going to assess (check) that your learners have understood what you have taught them, otherwise you will not know whether your methods have been effective or not. In each lesson you should:

○ review previous learning;

○ check instructions are understood;

○ check understanding of any new content introduced;

○ get learners to recap the lesson to check that key objectives have been achieved.

Summative assessment

It is part of a teacher's role to ensure that learners are well aware of summative assessment purposes and requirements well in advance of their final tests. Therefore you should:

○ raise awareness of available reasonable adjustments for learners with SEND, and negotiate individual requirements;

○ organise provision of such reasonable adjustments well in advance of the assessment;

○ check understanding of the format of the assessment;

○   check understanding of difficult words typically used in the assessment questions (rubric);

○   provide models of good practice to show the learners what success looks like, such as sample examination answers from previous papers or observations of professionals in the workplace;

○   give the learners opportunities for regular practice in test conditions; this can help make learners feel less nervous as they will be fully aware of the procedures, requirements and criteria.

Assessment throughout the teaching cycle

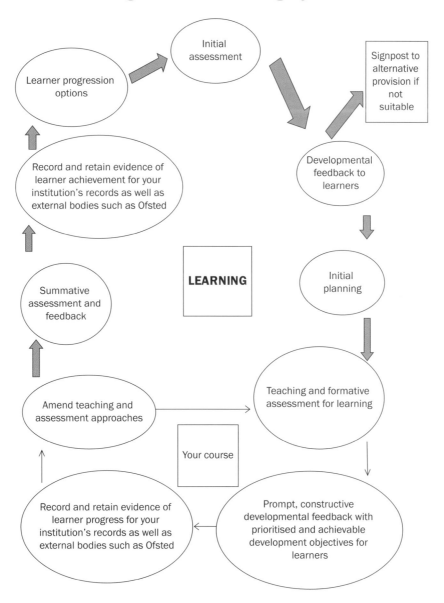

Figure 5.1 How assessment informs teaching and learning
Adapted from: Machin et al (2015).

KEY PRINCIPLES OF ASSESSMENT

It is unlikely that any assessment will ever be perfect in terms of fully meeting all of the following principles. Assessors should therefore strive to meet these principles as far as possible through close work with colleagues as well as the qualification's Awarding Organisation (AO).

Validity

Assessment validity is the extent to which the assessment approach effectively evaluates the required knowledge, skills and abilities in relation to the stated aim of the test. Put simply: does it test the knowledge and skills it is supposed to? This might sound obvious but there are always issues, relating to the further principles below, which may lessen an assessment's validity. For example, if a mathematics test has a time limit, it does not just test the learners' mathematics expertise but also their ability to think and work quickly. Similarly, any test which requires extensive writing is testing their literacy as well as the subject focus.

Reliability

Assessment reliability relates to its ability to be repeated without affecting learner outcomes. This is not easy as assessments such as exams have to be changed each time they are held, and will have different questions and even different content if the syllabus has been updated. It is difficult for assessors to set questions of equal difficulty for each cohort. Furthermore, assessors have to interpret criteria equally so that grades would be the same whoever performs an assessment. Similarly, any changes to the assessment environment can impact on the learners' ability to achieve. Therefore, any such changes to the assessment difficulty, inconsistency of assessors or differences in assessment conditions will reduce reliability.

Sufficiency

Assessments rarely cover all of the syllabus (content and skills) as this would be impractical. Therefore, sufficiency relates to the extent to which the key elements of the syllabus have been covered by an assessment.

Authenticity

Authenticity refers to the extent to which we can be sure that the learner is responsible for their own work.

Currency

Currency refers to the employability value of an assessment in terms of meeting the latest industry standards or national requirements and recognition within the relevant industry.

Case study

A plastering course uses a time-limited multiple-choice test to assess the knowledge and skills of its learners. Some of the learners complete the test online under strict time controls but due to a lack of available computers the rest of the class simultaneously complete a paper version of the test in a noisy workshop. Learners not present are given the test to take home and complete.

Activity

Consider what issues might make this assessment weak in relation to the key principles of assessment.

Comment

Your answer should have included some of the following points.

○   Assessors should always seek to minimise variation in the environment and conditions under which a test is set to help promote reliability in the outcomes. The impacts of the differing environments (IT room/workshop/home) and media used (IT/paper) would undermine this principle.

○   A multiple-choice test only assesses basic knowledge. It does not assess whether they can actually plaster competently and therefore would be of limited validity.

○   Having a time limit tests the ability to read quickly; a slow reader might have the necessary knowledge but not be able to complete the test on time, which questions the validity of the test in terms of it being a pure assessment of subject knowledge. Assessments are often timed for reasons of practicality as well as to develop employability skills of being able to work under pressure. However, the variance of practice shown in this case study makes its assessment unreliable as the students without a time limit are being judged on their subject knowledge only whereas the others are additionally being tested on their ability to work under pressure.

○   It would be hard for a teacher to invigilate the assessment in two locations, so learners might copy or look up answers. Allowing some learners to take work home also opens up the possibility of others helping them. Therefore, the assessment results may lack authenticity.

PRACTICES OF ASSESSMENT

Common assessment types and methods

There are a wide variety of assessment methods available for you to use. Remember that each one has differing advantages, challenges and limitations, so to gain an accurate and fair understanding of learners' abilities you need to use a variety of approaches. Table 5.1 summarises the common forms of assessment.

Table 5.1 Common methods of assessment

Assessment type	Advantages	Challenges and limitations
Teacher-led question and answer The teacher asks questions and a learner responds with the answer. The teacher praises the correct answer or corrects learner/asks other learners for the answer.	Enables quick and informal check of understanding before moving on to new content. Nominating learners enables you to grade questions to their ability and prevents some learners dominating the activity.	Only one learner at a time is active so your class could quickly become bored. If you ask a question to the whole class, rather than nominating, only the keenest will answer. This potentially disengages less confident learners from your class.
Examinations These formal assessments may be traditional paper-based or online.	As long as examination regulations are followed to prevent cheating, they guarantee authenticity; any other forms of assessment where work is completed outside such conditions run the risk of others helping the learner unfairly. These are usually timed, so they also test the ability to work quickly and under pressure. This is a useful skill for employment.	Timed assessments undermine the validity if the stated aim is purely to test subject knowledge; some learners underperform in pressure situations. The examination experience does not replicate realistic work experiences. It has limited validity in assessing practical competence for vocational subjects as it is difficult for examinations to assess learners' ability to apply their knowledge in the workplace.
Multiple-choice questions Learners select an answer from several possibilities.	Quick to administer and easy to mark, giving learners instant feedback on their progress. Usually focus on testing fact-based knowledge – where there is clearly a right or wrong answer so grading should be reliable.	Potentially limited validity as they do not assess the ability to apply knowledge in practical situations. Potentially limiting for more able learners as they tend to only test basic cognitive skills of knowledge and comprehension.

Table 5.1 (cont.)

Assessment type	Advantages	Challenges and limitations
Information closed questions Learners select from a list or think of the correct word to complete a text.	Computer-based assessments can select questions based on whether the learner is answering correctly or not, enabling them to be tailored to the learner's ability level. Many literacy and numeracy skills checks work on this basis so can be useful for initial assessment of learners prior to starting a course. Such assessments also give both teacher and learner instant feedback to inform future needs.	Where no list is provided, learners and markers need to be aware of issues such as whether accurate spelling is required or if there is more than one possible correct answer.
Open answer questions Assessments such as assignments may ask for learners' opinions on issues where there isn't a clear right or wrong answer.	These can be useful to stretch and challenge all learners as they provide the opportunity for answers to represent different levels of ability. These can also develop organisational and literacy skills.	Potentially time consuming to mark. Without clear right or wrong answers, there is a danger of subjectivity – where assessors apply the assessment criteria differently, meaning that the assessment lacks reliability.
Portfolios Portfolios of evidence enable the learner to build up evidence over the period of the course.	This potentially enables high sufficiency in terms of their ability to cover a large part of the course.	Compilation and marking might be time consuming, lack reliability and it may be difficult to guarantee the authenticity of the work.
Observation of practice Teacher observation of learners either in their workplace or a workshop environment in an organisation.	Allows you to assess learners' practical skills either in the workshop or workplace, giving potentially high validity and authenticity, especially for vocational subjects.	Observations are time consuming and costly to manage. Therefore, sufficient assessment coverage of the syllabus may be difficult.

Using technology to enhance assessment

Technology can be used to improve assessment processes in many ways.

○ Online tests through virtual learning environments promote learning out of the classroom.

○ Online multiple-choice assessments, where there is a clear right or wrong answer, allow automatic feedback and guidance regarding the appropriate level of future study.

○ A database provides instantly accessible information for teacher and institutional analysis. You can easily analyse which aspects of assessment your class, as well as specific individuals, complete successfully or unsuccessfully. Large-scale data collection and analysis will enable your organisation to identify specific groups in need of support and therefore target intervention to promote success for all learners.

○ More complex modelling/simulation programmes can promote deeper thinking through role playing and problem solving for both individuals and small groups of learners.

○ Use of differing technologies adds variety to the learner experience, helping to motivate further learning.

○ Technology can play a vital role in promoting equality of opportunity for learners with SEND as there are numerous enabling technologies available. Specialist hardware (equipment) and software (programs) can be used to help provide reasonable adjustments to support learners with SEND. For example, a learner with visual impairment may benefit from a specialist computer screen/magnifier or text-reading software. Seek guidance from your organisation's technical and SEND support teams, as well as the AO. Always negotiate with your learner which options best support their needs (see the following reasonable adjustments section).

Involving learners and others in the assessment process

Reasonable adjustments

Some learners may have Special Educational Needs or Disabilities (SEND). This means that you have a legal responsibility to make reasonable adjustments to support them to perform to the best of their ability. To help you with this:

○ investigate acceptable adjustments from your AO, such as extra time, provision of a reader or specified enabling technologies;

○ discuss needs and opportunities to make reasonable adjustments with the learner;

○ gain support and advice from your organisation's SEND co-ordinator, based on the SEND Code of Practice (DfE, 2015);

○ ensure that you report needs and adjustments to the SEND co-ordinator and/or management as required.

Most importantly though, never assume what will or won't work or what the learner needs; always discuss with your learner what support they find most effective for their personal development.

Self-assessment

Self-assessment is where learners evaluate their own abilities. This helps them to develop:

○ awareness of the assessment process;

○ responsibility for their learning;

○ skills of reflection for personal development;

○ raised personal aspirations of what they are capable of achieving.

Peer assessment

Peer assessment is where learners evaluate each other's work. As well as the benefits listed under self-assessment, peer assessment helps to:

○ develop communication skills;

○ promote a team ethic based around shared success;

○ provide an alternative source of feedback – learners may listen to peers more than teachers.

Possible disadvantages to self- and peer assessment include:

○ a lack of ability to judge own and others' work accurately;

○ a lack of maturity and/or ability to give constructive feedback, potentially leading to behaviour issues.

Self- and peer assessment must therefore be cautiously introduced to learners, with assessment expectations limited to what the learners are capable of judging, so start with getting them to assess simpler criteria first. Self- and peer assessment therefore tends to be used as formative assessment, helping learners to understand the assessment requirements prior to their final summative assessment.

Giving constructive feedback

Feedback refers to the information given to the learner in response to their assessment. It is one of the most effective learning tools, so it is important you get this right. A grade or a single mark might tell the learner how well they did in a test, but this gives them no idea how to improve. Effective feedback will lead to a learner adapting their approach to learning, so remember the word ADAPT to summarise this:

○ **A**ccurate – clearly show successes and areas for development;

○ **D**evelopmental – give clear, positive and constructive objectives for further improvement throughout the learning cycle;

○   **A**ssessed – carefully check learner understanding of your feedback. Complicated feedback using teacher language may not be understood and is therefore useless;

○   **P**rioritised – focus on the most important development needs;

○   **T**imely – regular feedback delivered shortly after the assessment tends to have the greatest impact on learning.

Making assessment decisions

To be as fair as possible, assessment judgements must utilise clear and consistently applied criteria. If a team of teachers are involved in assessment, standardisation should be implemented so that there is consensus regarding how criteria are interpreted, followed by moderation of assessments to check that teachers are marking to the same standard. In an assessment with high reliability, teachers would give the same grade for the same piece of work. To be a valid assessment, learners also need to understand how they are going to be judged. Following assessment they should also receive grading which transparently follows the assessment criteria, supported by indication of where, why and the extent to which these have or have not been met.

ASSESSMENT TO INFORM QUALITY ASSURANCE

Responsibilities and requirements

When teaching you are responsible for keeping accurate and up-to-date assessment records of your learners. This shows their current ability levels as well as the extent to which they have progressed during your course. The management of your institution as well as external quality bodies such as Ofsted will expect you to be able to produce these records on request to give evidence of learner progress. Such records also show the progress of learners and, where appropriate, others such as employers and parents, as well as giving an indication of likely final grades. You will need to carefully follow your institution's record-keeping guidance to help ensure compliance with their quality policies.

Prior to starting the course delivery, carefully check your assessment responsibilities and seek guidance within your organisation from assessment administrators. Carefully check the assessment regulations so that you are fully aware of what you have to do. For example, will you be responsible for administering any assessment, or is this organised by the AO? The AO will publish their regulations so it is vital that you carefully follow these to ensure reliability and fairness. For any areas of doubt, contact the AO well in advance of any summative assessments to ensure that you and your learners are appropriately prepared.

All qualifications in England and Northern Ireland are organised into levels from entry to level 8, with the latter representing a doctoral level of study. This used to be known as the Qualifications and Curriculum Framework, but since October 2015 it has changed to the Regulated Qualifications Framework (RQF) (Ofqual, 2015). According to Benson

(2015), the RQF aims to simplify assessment regulation by taking a less rigid approach, focusing more on the final outcomes of the qualifications rather than specifying their structure.

Legal issues, policies and procedures

As a teacher you may have to use potentially sensitive data such as information relating to disability to inform your assessment strategies. You will therefore have various legal responsibilities including adherence to the Data Protection Act (1998, amended 2011, cited in ICO, 2014). The use and storage of data by organisations is controlled by this Act, so ensure you understand and follow your organisation's data protection policy.

You have a legal responsibility under the Equality Act (2010, cited in EHRC, 2015) to ensure that learners are not unfairly discriminated against on the grounds of a disability or protected characteristics such as age or gender. The Act states that reasonable adjustments need to be made to ensure that learners with SEND have an equal opportunity to succeed. Equal opportunities therefore does not mean treating everyone the same but considering what reasonable changes to assessment procedures can be made to give everyone a fair chance of demonstrating their aptitude. Seek guidance from your AO regarding specific permissible adjustments to assessment procedure as well as support from colleagues responsible for working with learners with SEND (see the reasonable adjustments section above).

SUMMARY OF KEY POINTS

Assessment is a key part of your professional teaching practice. It is therefore vital that you consider how you will be assessing learners throughout the whole teaching and learning cycle. This means you need to:

o   make initial assessment as effective as possible;

o   incorporate formative and developmental assessment into your planning and teaching;

o   develop the self- and peer assessment capabilities of your learners;

o   give learners regular, prioritised and constructive feedback;

o   check that feedback is clearly understood and that learners know how to meet future objectives;

o   prepare learners for successful summative assessment without demotivating them;

o   effectively record formative and summative data;

o   learn from experience, data analysis and learner feedback.

Check your understanding

1   Explain the purposes of and differences between AfL and AoL.

2   What are the key principles of assessment?

3   What key principles of effective feedback can you ADAPT?

4   Why is accurate and up-to-date assessment record keeping important for you and your institution?

5   Outline three key points that you have learned from reading this chapter.

 TAKING IT FURTHER

Machin, L, Hindmarch, D, Murray, S and Richardson, T (2015) *A Complete Guide to the Level 4 Certificate in Education and Training.* 2nd ed. Northwich: Critical Publishing.

This is a key text if you wish to investigate any of the subjects covered in this book or intend to continue on to the CET. Chapters 3 and 4 give a more in-depth look at all aspects of assessment.

Tummons, J (2011) *Assessing Learning in the Lifelong Learning Sector.* 3rd ed. London: Sage.

This text specifically covers assessment in the FE sector.

Wiliam, D (no date). [online] Available at: www.dylanwiliam.org/Dylan_Wiliams_website/Welcome.html (accessed May 2015).

Dylan Wiliam's website on assessment. He is a key proponent of AfL. This site hosts key research as well as school-based practical ideas which you can adapt to help make assessment integral to your learners' development.

REFERENCES

Benson, J (2015) *Reforming Regulation of Vocational Qualifications.* [online] Available at: www.gov.uk/government/speeches/reforming-regulation-of-vocational-qualifications (accessed November 2015).

Black, P and Wiliam, D (1998) *Inside the Black Box: Raising Standards through Classroom Assessment.* London: King's College.

Department for Education (DfE) (2015) *SEND Code of Practice: 0–25 years.* London: DfE. [online] Available at: www.gov.uk/government/publications/send-code-of-practice-0-to-25 (accessed November 2015).

Education & Training Foundation (ETF) (2014) *Professional Standards for Teachers and Trainers in Education and Training – England.* [online] Available at: www.et-foundation.co.uk/supporting/support-practitioners/professional-standards/ (accessed June 2015).

Equality and Human Rights Commission (EHRC) (2015) *Further and Higher Education Provider's Guidance.* [online] Available at: www.equalityhumanrights.com/advice-and-guidance/further-and-higher-education-providers-guidance (accessed November 2015).

Information Commissioner's Office (ICO) (2015) *Guide to Data Protection.* [online] Available at: https://ico.org.uk/for-organisations/guide-to-data-protection/ (accessed November 2015).

Machin, L, Hindmarch, D, Murray, S and Richardson, T (2015) *A Complete Guide to the Level 5 Diploma in Education and Training.* Northwich: Critical Publishing.

Ofqual (2015) Homepage. [online] Available at: www.gov.uk/government/organisations/ofqual (accessed November 2015).

6 The microteach: using inclusive teaching and learning approaches

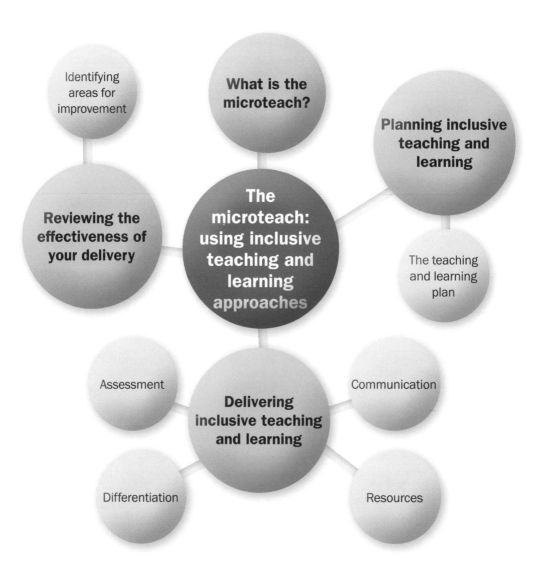

INTRODUCTION

This chapter prepares you in practical ways to tackle and succeed at the microteach.

OBJECTIVES

This chapter covers the learning outcomes of the following AET optional units (Group B, learning outcomes 3–5, level 3, 6 credits):

o   Understanding and using inclusive teaching and learning approaches in education and training (Education and Training unit).

The chapter therefore aims to develop your understanding and application of the following:

o   being able to plan inclusive teaching and learning;

o   being able to deliver inclusive teaching and learning.

See Table 1 at the front of the book to see how this chapter covers aspects of the ETF (2014) standards.

STARTING POINT

What do you already know about the microteach?

o   Do you know what you are required to do during a microteach session?

o   Do you know how long you will be observed for when you do your microteach?

Once you have some knowledge of what is required of you as a teacher, the natural next step is to explore how this can be put into practice. This is the role of the microteach.

WHAT IS THE MICROTEACH?

The microteach is an essential part of the AET. The microteach provides you with an opportunity to teach a brief lesson to your peers and to receive valuable feedback from them. It is the culmination of all of the aspects of teaching and learning that you will have studied while on your course and as explored in this book. It gives you an opportunity to put into practice your knowledge and understanding of:

o   roles and responsibilities (Chapter 1);

o   key aspects of inclusive teaching and learning (Chapter 2);

○ facilitating learning and development of groups and individuals (Chapters 3 and 4);

○ assessment (Chapter 5)

The AET requires that you are involved in *at least* 60 minutes of microteaching. This will usually comprise your own microteach of at least 15 minutes in addition to observation and participation in your peers' sessions of 45 minutes or more. Your institution will make a decision as to how and when this will occur although most likely this will be towards the end of the course.

> ## Activity
>
> What is the purpose of the microteach? Consider the potential benefits to you as a teacher.

○ The microteach is a safe environment in which you will gain the opportunity to demonstrate your emerging teaching skills.

○ You will be teaching a group of your peers on a subject that you know very well but without the pressures of a group of 'real learners'.

○ You will receive useful feedback from both your observer and peers in order to develop as a teacher.

The final point noted above is a key part of the microteach. Your tutor will observe your microteach session and provide you with written feedback, noting the strengths of the lesson and suggesting development areas.

PLANNING INCLUSIVE TEACHING AND LEARNING

The first step in planning your microteach is to identify a subject to teach. Some organisations will ask you to teach a session involving a subject related to your specialist area that you plan to teach in the future; however, many will leave the choice to you. Microteach sessions can involve teaching a wide range of subjects, from cake decorating, nail art, social media to dance and even bird song.

The teaching and learning plan

The content of your lesson will be documented on a teaching and learning plan which is an essential document in guiding your thoughts when planning your lesson. An example of such a plan is included in Appendix 3.

Your lesson should have a clear structure and the teaching and learning plan will guide you in achieving this. In order to achieve this structure it is useful to view the lesson as having three key parts: an introduction, main body and a plenary or summary activity to close.

One of the key elements of the teaching and learning plan is the aims and objectives section. An aim is a general statement of what the learners should gain from the lesson overall: for example, making a picture frame, evaluating the voluntary sector or exploring the history of chocolate. Objectives are formal ways to describe what you want the learners to be able to do or know at the end of the lesson that they could not do or did not know at the beginning of the lesson.

Once you have decided on the subject of your microteach, the next step is to consider what topics relating to this subject you want to include. The key purpose of a lesson of any kind is for learners to leave the lesson knowing something new or being able to do something that they could not do before.

Activity

Consider a microteach on the history of chocolate. What might you want the learners to learn from such a lesson?

If you were to teach a lesson on the history of chocolate you might want learners to learn about key dates in the history of chocolate, the different cultures and countries involved in chocolate production and perhaps the ingredients of chocolate too.

Once you have decided on your overall aim and what you want learners to learn you need to convert this into lesson objectives. You should share the objectives with the learners at the start of the session in order for them to have a clear insight into what they will gain from the session and draw on these at the end of the lesson to check learning has taken place.

When writing objectives you will need to draw on the SMART acronym:

S   **Specific:** The objective should state clearly what learners should gain from the lesson. It must contain an active verb and shouldn't include words like *know* or *understand*.

M   **Measurable:** Can achievement of the objective be measured via an appropriate form of assessment?

A   **Achievable:** Is the objective set at the right level?

R   **Relevant:** Is the objective relevant to what the learners have done in the lesson?

T   **Time-bound:** Objectives are usually time-bound to the current lesson – learners should be able to achieve the objective by the end of the lesson.

You should draw on these key elements when writing your objectives. To illustrate this further, consider the example of the history of chocolate. If learners are to learn about the key dates in the history of chocolate, the objective could be written with the use of *state* as the active verb, ie:

State at least three dates in the history of chocolate

You should avoid any general comments that are non-specific or difficult to measure by moving on from your general thoughts about what you want learners to learn to the specific objective. Some useful active verbs that you might want to use in writing your objectives are noted below.

describe   *list*   *explain*   *compare*   *analyse*   *evaluate*

Because these objectives are linked to gaining knowledge, they are used when referring to the cognitive domain (Bloom, 1956). Of course, these are not the only active verbs you can use, but they can guide you in the right direction.

Activity

What might the objectives be for the other two aspects of the lesson on the history of chocolate?

○   The different cultures and countries involved in chocolate production.

○   The ingredients of chocolate.

You might have thought that the learners could **describe** *the different cultures involved in early chocolate production*, or perhaps made it a little more challenging and asked them to **compare** *the different cultures involved in chocolate production.*

In addition to developing learners' knowledge, you may also want learners to develop skills or attitudes in your microteach lesson (see Chapter 2 for an exploration of the psychomotor and affective domains). If this is the case, you should still use active verbs in writing your objectives, though they will be representative of the domain used. Consider a microteach in which your broad idea is to increase awareness about the voluntary sector. The next step in planning is to consider what you want the learners to take away with them in terms of attitudes and perhaps knowledge too.

When writing your objectives in relation to attitudes – the affective (Krathwohl et al, 1964) domain – you may find the following active verbs useful:

challenges   *accepts*   *defends*   *argues*   *questions*

Activity

What might the objectives be for a microteach about the voluntary sector?

A microteach on the voluntary sector may involve an objective in relation to knowledge:

○   *List* five voluntary sector organisations.

It might also have an objective in relation to attitudes:

○ *Argue* for the importance of the voluntary sector in UK society.

When writing objectives for the skills that you want learners to gain this will require you to write your objectives in the psychomotor domain (Simpson, 1966). You may find the following active verbs useful:

build   *draw*   *paint*   *dance*   *assemble*   *perform*

Activity

What might the objectives be for a microteach that involves learners making a picture frame?

A microteach in which learners make a picture frame might involve an objective in relation to knowledge:

○ **Describe** *at least three types of woodworking joints that can be used in making a photo frame.*

It might also have an objective in relation to skills:

○ **Assemble** *the constituent parts of a photo frame and attach using wood glue.*

In addition to aims and objectives, your teaching and learning plan will also document the wider aspects of your lesson: your teaching and learning approaches as discussed in Chapter 2; your assessment methods as considered in Chapter 5 and also how these all come together to ensure both inclusivity for the learners and that individual learner needs are met.

DELIVERING INCLUSIVE TEACHING AND LEARNING

Your microteach is an opportunity to teach a very short lesson to your peers. It will allow your tutor to see the extent to which you have drawn together all of the elements of the course. On your teaching and learning plan you will need to note not only the sequence of events in your lesson but also the teaching and learning approaches that you plan to use.

 Case study

James is looking forward to his microteach session and has spent a long time preparing a presentation of 30 slides to share his passion for football with the group. He has set clear objectives and is confident in talking to the group.

Activity

What advice might you give to James to help him ensure that he engages learners through his microteach?

Comment

While a lecture or presentation element might be relevant to James' learners, he needs to use other teaching and learning approaches and limit the number of slides he uses. He might use a discussion, a group activity, a worksheet or even role play to engage the learners.

Differentiation

Throughout this book there has been an emphasis on the importance of meeting individual learner needs. Differentiation is an essential way of achieving this and is the approach taken when teaching, learning and assessment is planned with the individual, rather than the whole class, in mind. Differentiation can be undertaken in a number of ways, as noted in Table 6.1.

Table 6.1 Methods of differentiation

Method of differentiation	Explanation
Differentiation by task	Learners are provided with different tasks based on their current level or need
Differentiation by outcome	Learners at higher levels achieve higher level results from the same task
Differentiation by support	Additional support is offered to learners
Differentiation by setting or streaming	Learners at the same level are grouped together within a class or course
Differentiation by choice	Learners are given choices in a range of ways including the topics they consider, the products they create or the books that they read
Differentiation by resource	Different resources are provided to learners based on their level of achievement. This might include different texts or different handouts
Differentiation by learning style	Teaching, learning and assessment are tailored to the learning styles of learners

Assessment

You should draw on the key aspects of assessment during your microteach, remembering that assessment occurs throughout the lesson. You might be observing a group task, asking questions to check understanding or checking learners' participation in a group discussion. Your teaching and learning plan will have a section for you to note what assessment methods you are using and when.

Providing constructive feedback to learners to meet their individual needs

A key part of assessment is the importance of constructive feedback as discussed in Chapter 5. During your microteach session you should draw on these key principles, praising learners for correct answers to questions or when they do something well while also ensuring they know what to do to progress further.

Resources

The microteach is also an opportunity to explore resources that you can use to meet learners' individual needs.

Within a microteach, you might create a handout to support the lesson and enhance communication. You may possibly use presentation software, a flip chart or a wipe board. You might also use the tables and chairs in the classroom as a resource and move furniture to support your lesson.

Communicating with learners in ways that meet their individual needs

Communication is an essential skill for teachers. It may be verbal, to a whole group, small groups or to individual learners, or may be non-verbal and conveyed via smiles, nods or other representations of body language. Communication may also be visual and enhanced with images, handouts and presentation software.

Whatever methods of communication you use in your microteach session, you should ensure that they are effective. Clarity is important in any handouts that you use. You should make sure that the print is clear and the print size is suitable for all to read. For verbal communication think about the volume – loud enough for learners to hear, but not so loud that they are intimidated.

REVIEWING THE EFFECTIVENESS OF YOUR DELIVERY

Following your microteach you will be expected to evaluate your session, noting the strengths of the lesson, development areas and also what you might do differently if you were to deliver the session again. Being able to honestly reflect on what didn't go so well is a key skill for teachers. It is only by noting your development areas and suggesting what you might do differently that you will develop as a teacher.

Identifying areas for improvement

In addition to your tutor's feedback following the microteach lesson, you will probably receive feedback from your peers. This is an additional useful lens through which to view your teaching and it will help you in evaluating your lesson. Spend time looking through the feedback, noting if any key themes arise that you need to take account of which can help you develop as a teacher.

Having received feedback from your tutor and peers, you will now be able to draw on this and provide your own views and evaluation of the microteach lesson (see Table 6.2). When considering areas for development, you may find that it helps to think in terms of the ACTIV acronym (Assessment, Communication, Teaching and learning strategies, Inclusivity and Versatility).

Table 6.2 What to evaluate?

Assessment	What assessment methods did you use?
	Were the assessment methods effective?
	Could different methods be more effective?
Communication	Was your communication effective?
	(consider resources, voice, pitch, tone and communication with the whole class, individuals or small groups)
Teaching and learning strategies	What teaching and learning strategies did you use?
	Were the teaching and learning strategies effective?
	Could different teaching and learning strategies be more effective?
Inclusivity	Were all learners included in the session?
	Did you account for additional learner needs?
Versatility	Did anything unexpected happen? How did you adapt to overcome this?

SUMMARY OF KEY POINTS

This chapter has explored the importance of using inclusive teaching and learning and in particular:

○ planning an inclusive lesson that meets the needs of all learners;

○ using a range of teaching and learning strategies, communication methods, resources and assessment methods;

○ reviewing the effectiveness of a lesson to support your own professional development.

 Check your understanding

1 What is the purpose of a microteach session?

2 What are the three key parts a lesson should have?

3 When evaluating the effectiveness of a lesson, what does the ACTIV acronym represent?

4 What are three key methods of communication?

5 Whose feedback can you draw on when evaluating the microteach?

6 What are the three learning domains? What aspect of learning does each represent?

7 Outline three key points that you have learned from reading this chapter.

 TAKING IT FURTHER

Machin, L, Hindmarch, D, Murray, S and Richardson, T (2015) *A Complete Guide to the Level 4 Certificate in Education and Training.* 2nd ed. Northwich: Critical Publishing.

This is a key text if you wish to investigate any of the subjects covered in this book or intend to continue on to the CET. Chapter 5 gives a more in-depth look at all aspects of communication and Chapter 7 covers all aspects of planning and delivery.

REFERENCES

Bloom, B S (ed) (1956) *Taxonomy of Educational Objectives: The Classification of Educational Goals. Handbook I: Cognitive Domain.* New York: David McKay.

Education & Training Foundation (ETF) (2014) *Professional Standards for Teachers and Trainers in Education and Training – England.* [online] Available at: www.et-foundation. co.uk/supporting/support-practitioners/professional-standards/ (accessed December 2015).

Krathwohl, D R, Bloom, B S and Masia, B B (1964) *Taxonomy of Educational Objectives: The Classification of Educational Goals. Handbook II: The Affective Domain.* New York: David McKay.

Machin, L, Hindmarch, D, Murray, S and Richardson, T (2015) *A Complete Guide to the Level 5 Diploma in Education and Training.* Northwich: Critical Publishing.

Simpson, E J (1966) The Classification of Educational Objectives: Psychomotor Domain. *Illinois Journal of Home Economics,* 10(4): 110–44.

7 Essay writing

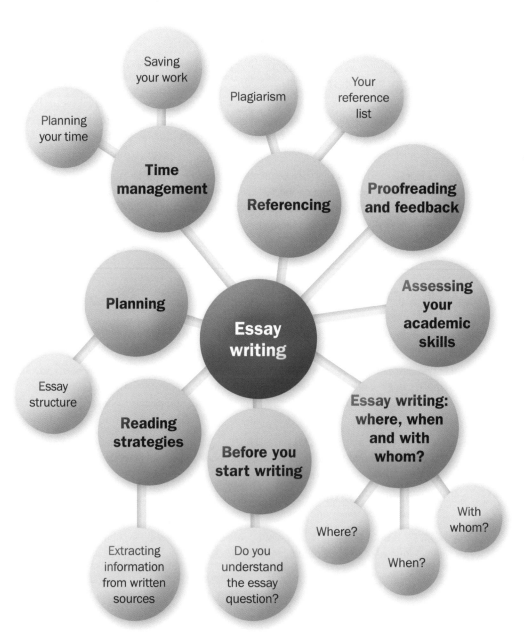

INTRODUCTION

As part of the AET you will need to complete assessments, including essays or extended pieces of writing. By developing your essay writing skills, this chapter helps you to present your knowledge and understanding in the best possible way. Doing this will also help you to step up to the next level of essay writing if you undertake a level 4 higher education qualification, such as the CET.

OBJECTIVES

This chapter covers the following learning outcome:

- understand how to develop your current essay writing skills.

The chapter therefore develops your understanding of the following:

- identifying any academic study skills that need developing;

- supporting you in your essay writing skills;

- progressing to the next level of essay writing skills needed for writing at higher education level.

See Table 1 at the front of the book to see how this chapter covers aspects of the ETF (2014) standards.

STARTING POINT

What do you already know about essay writing?

- Can you list at least three different components that make up an essay?

This chapter refers to 'essays' but your tutor on your AET course may use the term 'assignments'. Both are structured ways of presenting information that you have learned.

ASSESSING YOUR ACADEMIC SKILLS

Assessing your current essay writing skills before you need to write an essay and then preparing a plan to develop necessary skills is a good strategy to help you to complete your AET. Completing Table 7.1 and the exercises below will help you to do this. You will also find further information in the Taking it Further section at the end of the chapter.

Table 7.1 Assessing your own skills

Spelling, punctuation and grammar (SPAG)	Confident	Needs work
Common words spelled correctly		
Homophones spelled correctly (eg their, there and they're)		
Correct use of full stops and full sentences		
Correct use of capitals		
Correct use of tenses		
Subject-verb agreement (eg the <u>crowd is</u> big)		
Correct use of commas		
Correct use of apostrophes (especially omission, eg can't/cannot)	Avoid using contractions in academic essays	
Correct use of apostrophes (especially possession, eg Paul's box)		

Dura (2011)

Activity

When was the last time you wrote an essay? If you can find it, read it through along with any written feedback. Doing this will help to inform you of your strengths and weaknesses.

ESSAY WRITING: WHERE, WHEN AND WITH WHOM?

Where?

If you have not completed an essay for a while you may need to decide where the best place for doing this will be. Some people find it helpful to go to a library and work there, away from any distractions, and then to study for quite large chunks of time. For others, this is neither a choice nor a possibility and they will study from home. If you study from home, try to be in a different room, or away from the rest of your family. This may be the study or the bedroom or at the kitchen table. Try to make it as comfortable as possible. If you share the computer with other members of your family you might want to ask your educational establishment if they have a laptop that you can borrow.

When?

You may have little choice about what time you study because of your job, family and other responsibilities, but if you do have some choice try to decide when you work best. If you are a morning person, then it might be worth getting up before the rest of the family and grabbing some study time. If you prefer to work at night then do so but be careful about how it affects your ability to carry out other tasks during the day.

With whom?

Although the work you hand in has to be your own, there is no reason why you should not pair up with another person (or people) from the group and have a study group. It can be very motivational when you work alongside your peers but you do need to make sure you are not copying each other's work or always using the same references and sources of information.

BEFORE YOU START WRITING

It is important that you thoroughly understand your essay question and know what is expected of you by your tutor. Give yourself plenty of time to make sure that you have read the essay title and understand what it is you need to do. Ask yourself a number of questions:

- Do I have the assessment criteria?
- Do I know what the essay question is asking me?
- Do I know where to get extra information from to help with the essay?
- Do I know what the word count is?
- Do I know what layout is expected?
- Do I know the hand-in date?
- Do I know how or where to hand it in?
- Is there a cover sheet to complete?
- Do I put my name on it or a learner number?
- Do I know who my audience is, who I am writing for?

Only when you are comfortable that you know all of the answers should you start to work on the essay

Do you understand the essay question?

An essay will usually start with a verb asking you to do something, for example:

> ***Explain*** *how to promote equality and diversity in the classroom.*

Make sure you know exactly what the essay is asking you to do (such as: compare, contrast, identify). Your ability to identify what the essay question is asking you to do will become even more important when you move up to the next level of higher education writing.

Activity

Look up the words below in a dictionary and write in the definitions on a copy of the table below.

WORD	DEFINITION
Analyse	
Compare	
Contrast	
Define	
Describe	
Discuss	
Explain	
Identify	
Outline	
Summarise	

Highlight what you think are the key words in your first essay title for your AET and make sure you thoroughly understand all of those words. You could even rewrite the title in your own words; just make sure you do not stray too far from the original.

Essay title:

Key words:

Rewritten in your own words:

READING STRATEGIES

In order to write well you need to read well and also be able to take notes. This will help you to plan what you are going to write in your essay. Your tutor may give you most of what you need to read but it is always a good idea to do your own research and some additional reading. It is also good practice for the step up to level 4 (CET award) where you will have to do your own research and reference your work. You may have access to ebooks that you can access online or you may need to go to a physical library. Whatever sources you use in your essay, you may need to reference them so make sure that you take details of the book:

○   title;

○   author;

○   year published;

○   place of publication;

○   publisher;

○   web address (if online);

○   date you accessed it (if online).

Extracting information from written sources

Reading strategy 1 (DARTS)

Fluent readers often retain little of what they have read because they have developed the skill of skimming over the words to extract basic meaning. A set of strategies that you can use to extract and retain as much information as possible from a written source is 'directed activities relating to text' (DARTS). This is where you interact with the text in an active way to process and understand the text thoroughly.

Activity

o Underline: select a piece of text and underline words that are essential parts of it. (Do not write in a library book!)

o Tabulate: for each paragraph you read, write a short explanation of it in a table.

o Label: invent a title for each paragraph you read to illustrate its contents.

o Predict: predict what you think the next paragraph will be about, before reading it.

These strategies can be used with your learners as well; there are many DARTS activities for learners (see the Taking it Further section at the end of this chapter).

Reading strategy 2 (skimming, scanning and reading in depth)

Another reading strategy is skimming, scanning and reading in depth. We use these techniques without realising it in our day-to-day reading. Imagine you are reading a newspaper or a magazine.

o You scan over a page to find an article relevant to you.

o You skim through an article to get to the main points.

o You read in depth when you get to the main points you want to read.

You can use this strategy to quicken up your reading so you are only reading in depth the necessary parts.

PLANNING

Very few people can write a good essay without planning. Planning focuses your thoughts and ideas; developing your ability to do this will help you with your AET studies and when you go on to write higher level essays in the future. Crème and Lea (2008, p 74) identified a number of different types of essay writer:

   ○   the diver writer: the one that just needs to dive in and start writing and then the plan forms as they write;

   ○   the patchwork writer: writes in different sections then needs to stick it all together;

   ○   the grand plan writer: spends a long time thinking and making notes then writes it all out, more planned in mind than on paper;

   ○   the architect writer: plans the writing and has a strong idea of the structure before starting to write.

Activity

Which of the above do you think most closely describes you as a writer?

Write down a few lines about how you tackle an essay and then reflect on whether there are any strategies that you can adopt in order to improve this style.

Essay structure

An essay has a basic structure; this can help you to plan.

Introduction

Tell the audience what you will be writing about, say how you will go about it and define any specialist terms. It can sometimes be easier to write the introduction once you have finished the rest of the assignment. So, if you are struggling with how to start then go straight into the main body of the essay and come back to the introduction at the end.

If, as an example, the essay question asks:

Explain *how to promote equality and diversity in the classroom.*

Your essay introduction might start:

This essay will seek to explain how to promote equality and diversity in the classroom. First, it is necessary to define what the terms equality and diversity mean in terms of education.

Main body

Write about one main point in each paragraph. Each paragraph should address the question or part of the question. A good way is to think of each paragraph as if it were a mini essay on its own. Open with an introductory sentence outlining what the paragraph is going to be about and finish with a sentence that concludes by saying what was in the paragraph. The number of paragraphs will depend on the word count given.

If you take the same essay question as above:

Explain *how to promote equality and diversity in the classroom.*

Your main body structure might begin:

1. Start of first paragraph: *One way to promote equality and diversity in the classroom is to ensure that…*

2. Start of second paragraph: *Another way to promote quality and diversity in the classroom is to…*

Guide the reader through your work by signalling to them what you will discuss. Use starts of sentences such as:

○ *Turning to focus on equality*

○ *Looking at the learner's use of spoken English*

○ *With regard to the learner's use of literacy*

These signals should refer back to what you outlined in your introductory sentences. Spend time choosing your words carefully as it is easy to use words such as 'good' or 'things' which do not really aid clarity or understanding when expressing your ideas. Look for alternative words to help you express exactly what you want to say.

○ Each paragraph will have an introduction (point).

○ Each point will relate to the essay question.

○ Each point will tell the reader the topic of the paragraph.

○ Each paragraph will have a main body (evidence).

○ Your evidence will support your point.

○ Your evidence may include quotes, examples, statistics etc.

○ Each paragraph will have a final comment.

Your final comment will show how you have considered the evidence.

Your evidence may be strong:

○ *It is clear that…*

○ *It is without doubt…*

○ *It is evident that…*

Your evidence may be less strong:

○ *It is possible, therefore…*

○ *It is unlikely that…*

Conclusion

Summarise what you have written, come to a conclusion, if necessary, and show how it answers the question; never add any new evidence in the conclusion. Your introduction and conclusion, together, should give the reader a road map of the rest of your essay.

Table 7.2 A template for you to plan your first essay for your AET

Section	Points to write in this section
Introduction	
Main paragraph one	
Main paragraph two	
Main paragraph three	
Conclusion	

First draft

When you have completed your essay, consider it as your first draft and allow yourself time to read through it carefully while asking yourself the following questions:

1. Have you answered the essay question (compare, contrast, identify etc...)?

2. If you wrote an introduction, go back and see if you need to change it.

3. Are your arguments supported by evidence?

4. Are there any errors of grammar and spelling?

5. Could the writing style be improved?

6. Have all of the assessment criteria been met?

7. Does the conclusion match the paragraphs and the essay title?

TIME MANAGEMENT

Give yourself enough time to complete the assignment. Although you may hear of wonderful essays that have been written the night before, we're not sure how wonderful they can possibly be because adhering to some of the rules above will need more time than just 'the night before'. You certainly need time to read material before you sit down to tackle the essay. Once you have written your essay leave it alone for a few days. Coming back to your writing a day or two days later can prove invaluable for proofreading and restructuring, and remember that giving yourself plenty of time will help you when you move up to completing essays at level 4. Ask your tutor if you can look at a sample assignment from a previous group.

Planning your time

Whenever you get an assignment, set a goal for when you are going to start it so that you have the time to finish it without a last minute panic. Turla (2015) has some good tips for time management for learners; for example: once you are given a due date on an assignment, count backwards from this date to establish a start date. Take into account the time you will be spending on other things like social events, sports, etc; in addition, block out time on your calendar for other commitments. Book time on your calendar for completion of your assignment. Turla cautions you to remember the following:

○   *keep stress to a minimum;*

○   *start early to avoid a frantic finish;*

○   *if you usually wait until the last minute to study or work on an assignment, instead of making your goal to finish on time, make your goal to finish early.*

(Turla, 2015)

Saving your work

You will probably be required to type up your essay on a computer. It is always a good idea to back up a copy of your essay and any notes that you have made in a separate location from the computer you are using. Losing work due to computer error is not an acceptable reason for failing to hand in an essay on time. Having an online backup of your work is even more important if you use a laptop and carry it around with you as laptops can easily be lost or even stolen. You can access free online storage space through, for example, Dropbox, Google and Microsoft and doing this means that you can access your documents anywhere and on computers other than your own.

REFERENCING

Plagiarism

When you write a level 3 essay, you may be asked to reference your work. If not, then this section will be relevant when you progress to level 4 writing, where you will have to reference your work. When you read and take an idea from an author you should give them the credit for this idea, otherwise it is considered as plagiarism.

Activity

What steps can you take to avoid plagiarism?

Staffordshire University (2015) defines plagiarism as:

passing off someone else's work as your own. This can be research, statements, images and statistical data.

Staffordshire University (2015, p 1)

You can avoid plagiarism by referencing your sources. There are many different ways of referencing and your tutor will tell you which style you need to use. Many UK universities and colleges use the Harvard style of referencing; this method will be discussed in more detail below.

You only need to reference the books that you have actually used in your essay. When working at higher levels you will need to provide a bibliography. A bibliography includes all of the books and journals that you have read while researching an essay, even if you have not used them in the essay. This is because at a higher level you are expected to be influenced and informed by a wide range of reading even if you have not used this reading directly in your essay.

In the body of your essay you need to supply the author's surname and year of publication. You can either use the author's name as part of the sentence and then put the year in brackets. Alternatively, you can put both the author's name and the year of publication in brackets. Which method you use depends on whether the author's name forms part of the sentence or not (as in the examples below).

> ○   Single author:
>
> *Peart (2014) acknowledges that there are many challenges to maintaining a positive learning environment.*
>
> *There are many challenges to maintaining a positive learning environment (Peart, 2014).*
>
> If an author has published more than one document in the same year and you want to cite these you distinguish each document by adding lower case letters after the year within the brackets.
>
> *Peart (2014a) wrote about FE being the most diverse of the education sectors.*
>
> ○   Two authors:
>
> *In the book by Stork and Walker (2015)...*
>
> ○   More than two authors: write in full on first use and then cite 'et al' for further use:
>
> *Machin et al (2014) conclude that...*

Activity

Do you know what 'et al' means? If not, look up the meaning in a dictionary.

Your reference list

At the end of your essay you need to create a reference list of all of the sources that you have used. An outline of the information you need to compile a reference list is provided earlier in the chapter.

A BOOK

Black, P and Wiliam, D (1998) *Inside the Black Box: Raising Standards through Classroom Assessment*. London: King's College.

Machin, L, Hindmarch, D, Murray, S and Richardson, T (2015) *A Complete Guide to the Level 4 Certificate in Education and Training*. 2nd ed. Northwich: Critical Publishing.

AN EBOOK

Author, initials

(Year of publication)

Title. (Is it an edition? If so, this would go after the title)

[online]

Who published it?

Where was it published?

Available at: URL

(Accessed date)

Sadler, P (2003) *Strategic Management*. [online] Sterling: VA Kogan Page. Available at: www.netlibrary.com/reader/ (accessed May 2015).

WEBSITE

Author, initials (or website name if no author)

(Year of publication)

Title of website

[online]

Available at: URL

(Accessed date)

BBC News (2008) Factory gloom worst since 1980. [online] Available at: http://news.bbc.co.uk/1/hi/business/7681569.stm (accessed June 2012).

The reference list at the end of the piece of work needs to be in alphabetical order. See Taking it Further for a fuller guide to Harvard referencing.

PROOFREADING AND FEEDBACK

When you are proofreading your work, the level 1 and 2 SPAG (Spelling, Punctuation and Grammar) mark sheet from the Functional English marking criteria can be very useful (Dura, 2011). As literacy (as well as numeracy and ICT) is a key component of teaching and learning, it is a good idea for you to be familiar with the level 1 and 2 Functional Skills English Standards (Ofqual, 2012) to be able to help your learners in the classroom.

Each time you proofread, have something you are specifically looking for. Do not try to proofread everything at once. Proofread for content first.

- Does each sentence make sense on its own?
- Does each paragraph make sense on its own?
- Does the whole document make sense and answer the question?
- Will the educated non-specialist know what is being written about?
- Does the essay have a beginning, main body and a conclusion?

Then proofread for mistakes.

- Look for spelling mistakes.
- Check the spelling in the dictionary – do not rely on a spellchecker.
- Check for punctuation mistakes.
- Does a long sentence need rewording?
- Are apostrophes used correctly (possession and omission)?
- Does every sentence have a subject and verb?
- Are the verbs in the right tense? Have you changed tense halfway through a sentence or paragraph?

Activity

Go back to any previous essays to re-read the feedback and take on board any development points that your tutor or assessor has suggested.

Comment

Every time you write an essay, see it as an opportunity to improve by taking account of comments made on your previous essay and any tips or hints given by your tutor. If you do not understand any comments made or how to improve then ask your tutor for a tutorial – in plenty of time!

SUMMARY OF KEY POINTS

○ Time management.

○ How to plan.

○ An ability to skim and scan reading materials.

○ Proofreading (paying particular attention to SPAG) as well as an ability to remain focused on the essay task that you have been given.

○ Referencing.

 # Check your understanding

1 Why might you need to rewrite an introduction once you have finished your essay?

2 How do you use a possessive apostrophe with a plural noun?

3 What pieces of information do you need to be able to reference a book?

4 Can you use failure of technology as a reason to hand in an essay late?

5 Outline three key points that you have learned from reading this chapter.

 TAKING IT FURTHER

To find out more about Harvard referencing and plagiarism, this site is easy to follow but only explains Harvard referencing:

www.staffs.ac.uk/support_depts/infoservices/learning_support/refzone/plagiarism/index.jsp

See also:

www.staffs.ac.uk/assets/harvard_quick_guide_tcm44-47797.pdf

For classroom activities based around DARTS that you can use with your students, this is a good site but there are many others so search around for a level suitable for your students:

www.teachingenglish.org.uk/article/interacting-texts-directed-activities-related-texts-darts

This site will help you with your spelling, punctuation and grammar, if needed. It will also help you with your students, even if you are not teaching English:

www.bbc.co.uk/skillswise

An area that often causes problems is possessive apostrophes; to look further into this go to:

www.bbc.co.uk/skillswise/factsheet/en29punc-l1-f-apostrophes

For common-sense help about time management in a number of situations this site can be useful:

www.timeman.com/time-management-tips/time-management-tips-for-students

REFERENCES

Crème, P and Lea, M (2008) *Writing at University: A Guide for Learners*. 3rd ed. Berkshire: Open University Press.

Dura, M (2011) *Functional Skills Level 1 and 2 Spelling Punctuation and Grammar Mark Sheet*. [online] Available at: www.skillsworkshop.org/resources/functional-skills-level-1-2-spag-spelling-punctuation-and-grammar-mark-sheet (accessed December 2015).

Education & Training Foundation (ETF) (2014) *Professional Standards for Teachers and Trainers in Education and Training – England.* [online] Available at: www.et-foundation.co.uk/supporting/support-practitioners/professional-standards/ (accessed December 2015).

Ofqual (2012) *Criteria for Functional Skills Qualifications*. [online] Available at: www.gov.uk/government/uploads/system/uploads/attachment_data/file/371128/2012-01-16-criteria-for-functional-skills-qualifications.pdf (accessed December 2015).

Staffordshire University (2015) *Harvard Referencing – Guides and Examples*. [online] Available at: http://libguides.staffs.ac.uk/refzone/harvard (accessed December 2015).

Turla, P (2015) *Time Management Tips for Learners*. [online] Available at: http://timeman.com/time-management-tips/time-management-tips-for-students (accessed December 2015).

Glossary: the language of teaching

KEY TERM	DEFINITION
Assessment of learning	Making a clear judgement on a learner's subject-related knowledge and skills.
Assessment for learning	Identifying current knowledge and skills, future potential, and prioritised development needs.
Assessment-led learning	Over-assessment, to the detriment of learners' skills development and subject motivation.
Employability	The qualifications, skills and attitudes required to gain, maintain and develop a career.
Formative assessment	An assessment, often informal, which takes place throughout the learning process, with the aim of providing learners and teachers with an understanding of future development needs and priorities.
Regulated Qualifications Framework	A framework that provides equivalences between different types and levels of learning.
Summative assessment	An assessment, usually formal, at the end of a learning process which passes judgement on a learner's ability in the subject area.
Technology enhanced learning	The application of information and communication technology to teaching and learning.
In-service trainee	Enrolled onto a teacher training programme while employed in a teacher role.
Pre-service trainee	Enrolled onto a teacher training programme and provided with a training placement.
Problem-based learning	Learners learn through solving a problem relating to the subject.
Work-based learning	Learning the required skills for the job for which you are employed.

Appendix 1: Mapping the level 3 AET qualification with the LSIS units

In order to be awarded an AET qualification you need to achieve:

○   12 credits: this is the total credit value of the AET qualification.

These credits are made up of:

○   3 credits from the mandatory units in Group A;

○   9 credits from the optional units in Group B and Group C.

Some of the optional units require you to be teaching and for you to be observed in practice.

Unit title	Practice and observation requirement	Credits	Notes
Mandatory Group A			
Understanding roles, responsibilities and	No	3	This will allow trainee teachers to start on programmes and pass a unit without a practical teaching element
Optional Group B			
Understanding and using inclusive teaching and learning approaches in education and training.	Yes	6	For this optional unit there is a requirement to undertake microteaching for assessment purposes
Facilitate learning and development for individuals (Learning and Development unit)	Yes	6	This optional unit assesses occupational competence and requires trainee teachers to be assessed in a real work environment
Facilitate learning and development in groups (Learning and Development unit)	Yes	6	This optional unit assesses occupational competence and requires trainee teachers to be assessed in a real work environment
Optional Group C			
Understanding assessment in education and training (Education and Training unit)	No	3	This will allow trainee teachers to start on programmes and pass a unit without a practical teaching element
Understanding the principles and practice of assessment (Learning and Development unit)	No	3	This will allow trainee teachers to start on programmes and pass a unit without a practical teaching element

Learning Skills Improvement Services (2013, p 26) *Qualifications Guidance for Awarding Organisation: Level Three Award in Education and Training* (QCF).

Appendix 2: List of useful acronyms

Acronym	Full title
AO	Awarding organisation
ATL	Association of Teachers and Lecturers
BIS	Business, Innovation and Skills
CET	Certificate in Education and Training
CPD	Continuing Professional Development
CRB	Criminal Records Bureau
DBS	Disclosure and Barring Service
DET	Diploma in Education and Training
DfE	The Department for Education
DSL	Designated Safeguarding Lead
EHRC	Equality and Human Rights Commission
ETF	Education and Training Foundation
FE	Further Education
FELTAG	Further Education Learning Technology Action Group
HE	Higher Education
ICO	Information Commissioner's Office
ICT	Information and communication technology
IfL	Institute for Learning
ILP	Individual learning plan
ISA	Independent Safeguarding Authority
IT	Information technology
ITE	Initial Teacher Education
ITT	Initial Teacher Training
LLS	Lifelong learning sector

LSIS	Learning Skills Improvement Services
Ofqual	The Office for Qualifications and Examinations Regulation
Ofsted	Office for Standards in Education
PBL	Problem-based learning
PCET	Post-compulsory Education and Training
PGCE	Postgraduate Certificate in Education
QTLS	Qualified Teacher Learning and Skills
RQF	Regulated Qualifications Framework
SEND	Special Educational Needs and Disabilities
SET	The Society for Education and Training
SMART	Specific, measurable, attainable, relevant, time-bound
SoW	Scheme of work
SPOC	Single Point of Contact for Prevent
TES	Times Educational Supplement
TEL	Technology enhanced learning
UCU	University and College Union
VAK	Visual, auditory, kinaesthetic
VARK	Visual, auditory, read/write, kinaesthetic
VLE	Virtual Learning Environment

Appendix 3: Teaching and learning plan template

Teaching and learning plan

Teacher:	Number of learners:	Date:	Time:

Resources:

Lesson aim:

Objectives:

Equality and diversity / inclusivity:

Time	Teacher activity	Learner activity	Assessment	Resources

Index

Available now

CRITICAL
PUBLISHING

A Complete Guide to the
Level 4 Certificate in Education & Training

SECOND EDITION

LYNN MACHIN, DUNCAN HINDMARCH,
SANDRA MURRAY & TINA RICHARDSON

FURTHER
EDUCATION

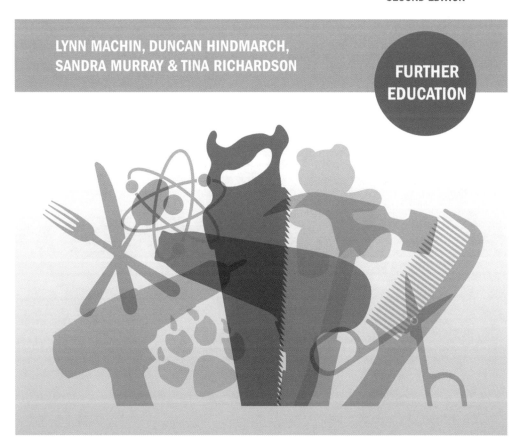

New edition coming soon

CRITICAL
PUBLISHING

A Complete Guide to the
Level 5 Diploma in
Education & Training

SECOND EDITION

LYNN MACHIN, DUNCAN HINDMARCH,
SANDRA MURRAY & TINA RICHARDSON

FURTHER
EDUCATION